Writings of Healing
and Resistance

5-22-14

TO: JANET
You HAVE An AMAZing
ViBe. Thanks for
Listening to me —
Thanks for supporting
our first
"A DAY of Color "
PEACe,

Mary

Cultural Critique

Norman K. Denzin
General Editor

Vol. 7

The Cultural Critique series is part of the Peter Lang Education list.
Every volume is peer reviewed and meets
the highest quality standards for content and production.

PETER LANG
New York • Washington, D.C./Baltimore • Bern
Frankfurt • Berlin • Brussels • Vienna • Oxford

Writings of Healing and Resistance

Empathy and the Imagination-Intellect

Edited by Mary E. Weems

PETER LANG

New York • Washington, D.C./Baltimore • Bern
Frankfurt • Berlin • Brussels • Vienna • Oxford

Library of Congress Cataloging-in-Publication Data

Writings of healing and resistance: empathy and the
imagination-intellect / [edited by] Mary E. Weems.
p. cm. — (Cultural critique; v. 7)
Includes bibliographical references.
1. Empathy. 2. Self-consciousness (Awareness)
3. Group identity. I. Weems, Mary E.
BF575.E55W75   152.4'1—dc23   2012038449
ISBN 978-1-4331-1208-9 (hardcover)
ISBN 978-1-4331-1209-6 (paperback)
ISBN 978-1-4539-0885-3 (e-book)
ISSN 1530-9568

Bibliographic information published by **Die Deutsche Nationalbibliothek**.
Die Deutsche Nationalbibliothek lists this publication in the "Deutsche
Nationalbibliografie"; detailed bibliographic data is available
on the Internet at http://dnb.d-nb.de/.

Cover design by Pauline Sameshima
Author photo by Jim Lang

The paper in this book meets the guidelines for permanence and durability
of the Committee on Production Guidelines for Book Longevity
of the Council of Library Resources.

© 2013 Peter Lang Publishing, Inc., New York
29 Broadway, 18th floor, New York, NY 10006
www.peterlang.com

Printed in the United States of America

This book is dedicated to my maternal grandparents

Mary Isabel and Sylvester Lacy

All of the ancestors I don't know about thanks to Slavery

My husband, James E. Amie, Jr.

And the authors whose work

is included in these pages

thank you.

Contents

Introduction
Hope, Pedagogy and the Imagination-Intellect

Norman K. Denzin

It is an honor to welcome this new book by Mary Weems into our Peter Lang Series. As she did in her earlier book, *Public Education and the Imagination-Intellect: I Speak from the Wound in My Mouth*, Mary offers a creative tour de force, a rich multi-layered text, working across multiple genres and multiple points of view. She challenges us to go more deeply into the dark places of schooling and public education. She moves her imagination-intellect theory into the spaces of emotion, affect, and feeling. In so doing she extends her insights into the key notions of aesthetic appreciation, oral expression, written expression, dramatic performance, and social consciousness.

She believes that the language arts are a powerful way to counter apathy and encourage empathy. She believes that there will be justice and love in the world if they could only be nourished in our schools, families, and communities. For Mary empathy and emotional understanding are grounded in a critical social consciousness: creating this critical consciousness should be a primary goal of public education. In this way we can move closer to a socially just democratic society, which is not yet yet.

The Imagination-Intellect as a Pedagogy of Freedom

Within this framework, extending Freire (2000), Mary's imagination-intellect contributes to a conception of education and democracy as pedagogies of free-

dom. As praxis, the imagination-intellect is a way of acting on the world in order
to change it. Dialogic performances, enacting a performance-centered ethic, provide materials for critical reflection on radical democratic educational practices.
In so doing, performance and art enact a theory of selfhood and being. This is
an ethical, relational, and moral theory. The purpose of the particular type of
relationality we call research ought to be enhancing...moral agency, moral discern-
ment, critical consciousness, and a radical politics of resistance.

Following Freire. praxis is a defining feature of human life and a necessary
condition of freedom. Human nature is expressed through intentional, meaningful conduct that is anchored in historically specific situations. The desire for
freedom is basic. People make history and culture through their performative acts,
and these acts enable the realization of freedom, the opening up of choices, often
in the face of oppression and resistance. Freedom is never given. Race, class, and
gender oppressions limit human agency and the freedom to act in a given way.
Freedom is always contingent—contingent on a pledge to struggle and resist, on a
willingness to accept the consequence of one's actions. The practice of democratic
freedom requires a condition of permanent struggle, the promise to transform the
world in the name of freedom itself.

A position of militant nonviolence is paramount. The struggle for freedom
and for democracy must honor human life. Violence is never justified. A commitment to nonviolence structures struggles of liberation, and these struggles always occur within contested terrains. In turn, the permanent struggle for freedom
and liberation gives to "all equally the power to seek self-determined hopes and
dreams" (Glass, 2001, p. 23). Performance ethnography performs these struggles
and becomes, in the process, the practice of freedom itself.

Indeed, performance ethnography grounded in the ways of the imagination-
intellect enters the service of freedom by showing how, in concrete situations,
persons produce history and culture, "even as history and culture produce them"
(Glass, 2001, p. 17). Performance texts provide the grounds for liberation practice
by opening up concrete situations which are being transformed through acts of resistance. In this way, performance ethnography advances the causes of liberation.

Hope

As an interventionist ideology the critical imagination is hopeful of change. It
seeks and promotes an ideology of hope that challenges and confronts hopelessness. It understands that hope, like freedom, is "an ontological need." Hope is the
desire to dream, the desire to change, the desire to improve human existence.
Hopelessness is "but hope that has lost its bearings" (Freire, 1999, p. 8).

Hope is ethical. Hope is moral. Hope is peaceful and non-violent. Hope
seeks the truth of life's sufferings. Hope gives meaning to the struggles to change

the world. Hope is grounded in concrete performative practices, in struggles and interventions that espouse the sacred values of love, care, community, trust and well-being (Freire, 1999, p. 9). Hope, as a form of pedagogy, confronts and interrogates cynicism, the belief that change is not possible or is too costly. Hope works from rage to love. It articulates a progressive politics that rejects "conservative, neoliberal postmodernity" (Friere, 1999, p. 10). Hope rejects terrorism. Hope rejects the claim that peace comes at any cost.

The critical democratic imagination is pedagogical in four ways. First, as a form of instruction, it helps persons think critically, historically, sociologically. Second, as critical pedagogy, it exposes the pedagogies of oppression that produce and reproduce oppression and injustice (see Freire, 2000, p. 54). Third, it contributes to an ethical self-consciousness that is critical and reflexive. It gives people a language and a set of pedagogical practices that turn oppression into freedom, despair into hope, hatred into love, doubt into trust. Fourth, in turn, this self-consciousness shapes a critical racial self-awareness. This awareness contributes to utopian dreams of racial equality and racial justice.

Mary and her collaborators chart a pathway through these critical spaces. They write with power and passion. They take us into and through the fields of abuse—bruised spirits, the wounded body, the kindness of medical strangers, the poetics of black mother-womanhood, violence against black women, mothers and their sons, silenced black voices, post-racial classrooms. These writers have the unique ability to make their own and other's experiences come alive. This is a frame-breaking book which will have a profound effect on the field of critical inquiry.

References

Freire, Paulo. (2000). Pedagogy of the oppressed, 30th anniversary edition, with an Introduction by Donaldo Macedo. New York: Continuum.

Freire, Paulo. (1999). Pedagogy of hope. New York: Continuum. (originally published 1992).

Glass, Ronald David. (2001). On Paulo Freire's philosophy of praxis and the foundations of liberation education. Educational Reseacher, 30: 15–25.

One Love
Empathy and the Imagination-Intellect

Mary E. Weems

Empathy is more important than ever to a national population worried about difficult political and socioeconomic situations. During the last 10 years, an enormous amount of research has been carried out to elucidate the nature, mechanism, and function of empathy. New research from social-cognitive neuroscience and related fields indicates that, like language or eye-hand coordination, empathy is an innate human capability that can be greatly enhanced by purposeful and informed guidance.
—Karen E. Gerdes and Elizabeth A. Segal (2011, p. 141)

When the power of love overcomes the love of power, the world will know peace.
—Jimi Hendrix

During the first semester of my doctoral work in Education, I was concerned that reading and writing in what I define as dense "academese"-filled scholarship would hamper my ability to write creatively. I asked: When I write in traditional scholarship, do I stop being a poet? This question ultimately led to the development of my imagination-intellect theory. For a full discussion of this theory including its connection to the work of John Dewey, Maxine Greene, Paulo Freire, and others, as well as the artists of the Harlem Renaissance and Black Arts Movements who used their work as what Gordon Parks called his "choice of weapon" (1986), see my *Public Education and the Imagination-Intellect I Speak from the Wound in My Mouth* 2003). What I didn't include at the time is any reference to what my slave ancestors and people like W.E.B. Du Bois knew and what bell hooks (1994), Theresa Perry (2003) and others know: education is the practice of freedom, and everything I do as an artist-scholar is informed by this fact, even in the midst of continued injustice and oppression.

The imagination-intellect theory has five components: aesthetic appreciation, oral expression, written expression, dramatic performance, and social consciousness. I made two brief references to the importance of empathy in my *I Speak* text, the first echoing Maxine Greene (1995), who believes that "our ability to empathize is linked to our capacity to imagine, it is what allows us to envision alternative realities" (Weems, 2003, p. 7), and the second from my own perspective: "The arts are a powerful way to counter apathy and encourage empathy. I nurture this path to the Golden Rule in my own life through social consciousness, creative-critical thinking, and performance (2003, p. 101). After several years of teaching as a part-time and full-time faculty member, I thought about all of the scholarship and art that's been created which argues for better public schools, more qualified teachers, a more balanced and culturally diverse curriculum, and a better world. I thought about all the people who practice religions that emphasize love for each other, compassion, and mercy, as well as all of the people who have earned college degrees in disciplines that emphasize social justice and a true participatory democracy.

I asked: Why isn't this world in a better social position in terms of the way we treat each other? This question, coupled with my continued conscious effort to become more empathetic through the language arts and to push my students to do the same, led to the conclusion that social consciousness is the component of my theory in which the ability to empathize or more closely identify with people from different or *othered* backgrounds occurs, and that self-exploration through the other four components is one way of becoming more empathetic. Just as artists work in various mediums, each with his or her own process for sharing thoughts and feelings about a particular topic or moment, individuals may get to the same place I define as empathy: a deep, spiritual, close identification with the experiences of the other in a way that works for them. I began to expand this theory in two previous publications, "Food for Thought: The Imagination-Intellect and the Role of Empathy (2009a) and "The E in Poetry Stands for Empathy" (2009b). Consider this slightly revised excerpt from "Food for Thought":

> Unlike traditional notions of cognition that relegate thinking to various dichotomous parts, and posit that the process for artists is from a more emotional, subjective perspective while scientists are rational, objective thinkers, I believe cognition is the same process for artists and scientists. A visceral metaphor for the imagination-intellect would be to consider the imagination, where new ideas come from as representing the heart and the intellect, the knowledge base that helps us synthesize information, get new ideas, and think things through as the

arteries, veins, and capillaries. Thinking is a fluid, inextricably linked process mirroring "blood" as it circulates through the body.

My imagination-intellect theory (see Weems, 2003), incorporates Maxine Greene's aesthetic appreciation and aesthetic expression (oral and written), as well as dramatic performance and social consciousness. The imagination-intellect is informed by the seamless flow between the way a person thinks and how they feel emotionally. It is not possible to have an idea without drawing upon the intellect. It is not possible to think without feeling. Facilitating imagination-intellect development should be the primary goal of public education. This includes helping all students become more socially conscious by understanding their social position, the real history of America, the connection between thinking and feeling, and the importance of struggling for a more just, inclusive democratic society. (2009a, p. 150)

Later in this chapter I will describe the spiritual process of creating from the space between consciousness and unconsciousness. As part of this process, I borrow from my background in English to describe how I experience degrees of empathy based upon the use of the first, second, or third-person point of view. Finally, just before I share several exemplars of empathic writings, I state that I'm not suggesting that there is one way of developing empathy. Rather, I'm sharing what the process is like for many students and me and others I've encouraged to pursue a more empathic way of being in the world (2009a).

How do I know this method for exploring empathy works? Because of the countless examples in my own work over the last several decades both prior to and after the construction of this theory, the work of other artists working across various mediums I've engaged where the empathy for their subject has been evident, and the work of hundreds of college students who have experienced my performance-based, empathy-driven midterms. Since Social/Cultural Foundations of Education is by design interdisciplinary, I originally intended to conduct a review of the current literature referencing empathy in Education, History, Anthropology, and English (the areas that most intersect with my own research), but the majority of the work I reviewed was written by scholars working in various sub-disciplines of psychology.

This is not a "complete" or all-inclusive review of the definitions of empathy, because the body of work across disciplines is extensive and growing. The focus of this chapter is my own definition of empathy and how it informs social consciousness, the fifth component of my imagination-intellect theory, including examples from my work, how my definition compares to how it's defined by other scholars, and a discussion of the performance-based midterm projects students complete in my Multicultural Education classes, including three recent examples of their work.

The overwhelming majority of the scholars in this review of the literature defined empathy either specifically or by description as affective and/or cognitive, loosely defined as either the ability to feel the same as the "other" or to think the same as the "other." In most cases the authors note that it's possible to experience affective and cognitive empathy separately, and in a few instances what I consider the inextricable connectedness of the process is described by researchers working in Child Psychology, Educational Leadership & Psychology, Social Psychology, Psychology, Medicine, Curriculum and Instruction, Political Psychology, English, Psychology, Neurology, Dentistry, Anesthesia, Social Work, Educational Psychology, Reading, Nursing, Social and Clinical Psychology, Social Psychology, and Social Psychology respectively (Ang & Goh, 2010; Barr & Higgins-D'Alessandro, 2009; Batson et al., 2002; Caravita & Di Blasio, 2009; Exline & Zell, 2009; Gladstein, 1983; Hojat, 2009; Knight, 1989; Lane, 2001; Lindquist, 2004; Loggia et al., 2008; Lu et al., 2005; Maxwell & DesRoches, 2010; Meek, 1957; Morgan & York, 2009; Panosky & Diaz, 2009; Rangganadanan & Todorov, 2010; Rumble et al., 2010; Sams & Truscott, 2004).

Like Vygotsky (1978, 1986) who—as Bridget Cooper, veteran classroom teacher and professor of Education, notes—"stressed the role of human relationships in learning and highlighted the separation of affect and cognition as a key failing of psychology" (2010, p. 82), I disagree with the separation of empathy into affective and cognitive domains as if this is the way empathy is actually experienced. Barr and Higgins-D'Alessandro agree when they define it as a "[s]et of related constructs with emotional and cognitive components: 1) Perspective taking, an individual's ability to view situations from a third-person perspective by [considering] one's own and others' subjective perspectives, 2) Emotional components, feelings of warmth, compassion, concern for others…" (2009, p. 752).

Since the history of education informs my work, I was surprised when I read in Brooks's (2009) "Historical Empathy in the Social Studies Classroom: A Review of the Literature" that there is little consensus regarding what "historical empathy" means and that this "confusion is only compounded by the tendency of some to ignore previous theoretical arguments and research findings in their own work" (p. 214). In her review, Brooks shares several often-conflicting definitions, then points out that Foster and Yeager, "who have contributed a great deal to this discussion" (p. 214), define historical empathy as the "ability to infer from given knowledge an explanation of certain actions" (p. 215). According to Brooks, for Foster and Yeager "historical empathy combines the adductive and logical thinking associated with use of evidence" with "the inferential and appropriately creative skills that seek to bridge the gap between what is known and what may be inferred from history. This conceptualization identifies empathy as a cognitive process necessarily embedded in the historical method" (p. 215).

In spite of the lack of consensus on one definition, Brooks (who does not offer her own definition in this article) "in another action research study sought to determine the impact that different types of commonly used writing assignments might have on [eighth-grade] students' ability to display historical empathy"

(2009, p. 227). After sharing "primary and secondary sources," she "alternately assigned first and third person writing exercises" (p. 227). She concluded that first-person writing "invite[d] inferential thinking [and] was...more likely to include decontextualized thinking about the past...[while] third person writing... appeared to focus students' attention on the accuracy of information as it detracted from propensity to make inferences" (pp. 227–228). In her study Brooks concurs with what I discuss regarding degrees of empathy in "Food for Thought":

> There are degrees of empathy. Each attempt reaches its own limit without conscious thought—the idea is to focus on a level of spiritual opening that happens when the mind, body, and spirit are communicating as one. The level of empathy changes each time an individual has an encounter. When I'm inspired to write in the first person, I'm engaged in feeling-thinking at an intimate level because during the creation process, I come closest to standing in the space of another. This is not to suggest that all first person writing means that the author is purposely engaging the experience of the other—I'm bearing witness to my experience.
>
> When I write in second person as if I'm close enough to witness what's happening, the connection is not as deep because for reasons I'm currently unable to articulate, a first person connection does not happen. In third person, the distance between the individual, or social issue and me broadens as I (not purposely) find myself outside the situation further limiting the level of empathy achieved. Any increase in the ability to empathize represents progress, and the years I've spent honing this ability have resulted in a heightened desire to find part of myself in everyone else.
>
> In all cases, when I'm writing from outside a particular race, ethnicity, or social experience, I'm not writing or speaking *for* the person or group, or as an expert on whatever the social issue is. Nor am I suggesting that what I write will mirror someone else's lived experience. I'm trying to get close enough to better identify with a situation I've never lived happening to someone else. (2009a, p. 153)

Following her analysis of her students' work, Brooks discovered that writing in the third person took the students' attention away from empathizing as much as they did when writing in the first person. As I discuss in the above quote, I've realized this about my own empathic writings as well as the performance-based, empathetic midterms of my students. Brooks concludes by sharing that "researchers cited here cited other definitions of Historical Empathy but did not consider how they connected or disconnected to their own, resulting in a disjointed conversation about student development of historical empathy" (p. 218). Brooks also points out that according to Cunningham (2009), "most historical Empathy scholarship has focused on students' thought processes, not on teacher knowledge or pedagogy" (p. 218).

Hollan and Throop's (2008) review of the literature in anthropology reached the same conclusion as Brooks's review of historical empathy, pointing out that "although many anthropologists…presume the importance of empathy in social life and field work, only a handful have been explicit about defining…it" (p. 385). They continue by sharing that "[e]ven the definition of empathy remains unsettled for anthropological purposes." *Webster's Seventh New Collegiate Dictionary* (1967) defines empathy as "1: the imaginative projection of a subjective state into an object so that the object appears to be infused by it" and "2: the capacity for participating in another's feelings or ideas" (p. 386).

Throop continues:"How do we account for [empathy's] relative absence in the anthropological discussion? Part of the answer [is] Geertz's (1984) critique… [in which] he used the failure of anthropologists…to distinguish clearly between empathy and projection to challenge the idea that gaining first-person-like knowledge of others involves any kind of special experiential or emotional component" (p. 388). Throop concludes that for Geertz, "too often…the anthropologist who presumes she is being 'empathetic' is merely projecting her own thoughts and feelings onto…the subjects of study" (p. 388).

I disagree with Geertz. The body of empathic work I've created, which others have found deeply empathetic, counters his position, because while my lived experiences may unconsciously inform the work in some way, the details I create and the thoughts and feelings my writing convey are coming from a sacred, spiritual space between the conscious and unconscious. Also, the experiences and/or social issues I'm consciously attempting to empathize with are not my own, and I'm often surprised by what's written. For these reasons, it's much too simplistic to suggest that I'm merely "projecting my own thoughts and feelings onto…the subjects of study" (p. 388). Further, the midterm writings, performances, post-midterm reflections and discussions I've facilitated with students over the past 15 years counter Geertz's position.

Other types of empathy include Profound Empathy (Cooper, 2010), Moral Contours of Empathy (Carse, 2005), Narrative Empathy (Moore & Hallenbeck, 2010), Intergroup Empathy (Chiao & Mather, 2010), Ethnocultural Empathy (Rasaol, et al., 2009), and Realistic Empathy (Schwebel, 2006).

In addition to what I've just discussed, I learned three things during this review: (1) Each scholar has his or her own way of defining empathy, including terms and language choices, making it difficult if not impossible to develop one universal definition even within disciplines; (2) In each instance a process for developing empathy is discussed that is unique in terms of number of steps and the way each is described; (3) The importance of empathy is evident in the abundance of scholars exploring this phenomenon in their work.

I end this brief review of some of the literature regarding empathy with a quote from Peter L. Fischl, a holocaust survivor whom Gorrell (2000) invited to speak to her English class: "The most important thing is…I want to help people start to think and to educate themselves and to love each other, so no one ever has to go through what that little Polish boy went through again" (p. 32).

Gorrell's class was based on a peace curriculum and confirms the Jimi Hendrix quote that began this chapter: "When the power of love overcomes the love of power, the world will know peace." Being disconnected from our humanity, from our ability to empathize or closely identify with the lived experiences of another, flies in the face of what it means to *be* fully alive, living in the moment, concerned about other people and their plight—consciously considering their connection to our own mortal selves. The resultant commitment to live objectively rather than subjectively makes it easier to objectify the other in the name of reason, individuality, and survival of the fittest.

Over the years, most of the people I've asked about their ability to empathize have claimed that it's not possible until they make a serious, conscious attempt to try it with my guidance. Even first attempts often surprise the person who's completed the exercise. In terms of the *haves* versus the ever-increasing number of *have-nots*, too many people in this world are operating based upon the idea that the mind and body are separate, that thoughts and feelings occur separately rather than simultaneously, that to attempt empathy is at best a long shot more akin to sympathy or compassion, because even getting close to standing in the shoes of another is impossible. I disagree.

The December/January 2012 issue of *Time* magazines elected "The Protester" as "Person of the Year." Following the spark lit by the Occupy Wall Street movement last September, men and women all over the world, including countries such as Tunisia, Egypt, Libya, Yemen, and Bahrain, are rising up to "occupy" the streets while fighting against *the haves* for human rights (pp. 54–61). These ongoing, historical events, sparked in part by a desire for democracy, religious and economic change, and equality for women, highlight the need for a global, social consciousness grounded in empathy. The following examples indicate the power of the imagination-intellect theory in practice.

Here I share three empathic writings, "Rainwater," "Fortune 500," and "Haiku," followed by a brief discussion of my performance-based midterms. I end with a graduate student's introduction to the final section, which includes her midterm and the midterms of two undergraduates.

1. Empathy with What It Means to Be Young, White, and Lesbian

"Rainwater"

(Young lesbian [20s–early 30s] enters from stage left, wearing a rainbow tie-dyed t-shirt, a short jean skirt, red high-topped tennis shoes, and white socks, playing/reciting:)

The itsy bitsy spider crawls up the water spout, down came the rain and washed the spider out, out came the sun and dried up all the rain and the itsy bitsy spider crawled up the spout again (PAUSE, facing audience, crouching)

I tried to kill a spider once, really I was practicing....I kind of felt like that spider most of the time, caught in my own web, not sure what I'm doing there, wanting freedom, not knowing what that was. [PAUSE] When I was a kid I spent hours and hours watching them...my mom and dad were true gardeners, and spiders loved the flowers, and vines, and short green bushes, they nurtured each year. [SHE STANDS AND LOOKS AROUND, SEEING THEIR GARDEN] One morning after a rain I caught one and kept dunking it in a styrofoam cupful of water...each time I'd hold it down longer, and each time it would sit there as-if-dead for about 30 seconds and then it would start to move. [PAUSE] I decided you can't kill a spider with rainwater—that maybe being caught in your own web wasn't so bad—that the spider "did" know what it was doing there.... [PAUSE] I'm gay.... Yep, a lesbian if you want to be correct—I've heard all those other words too—even from my own...family but I've learned that I'm a spider—that rainwater is cleansing, I can't drown in it—I only start drowning when I'm not being myself. [PAUSE]

My father's brother, I used to call him Uncle Herman, knew before anybody—even me. When I was nine my parents left me with him one day while they went to a friend's funeral. He'd always been nice to me, bringing me my favorite spearmint gum, Hershey bars, and once a brand new Powerpuff girl house. [PAUSE] That day, I was in the garden watching a spider make a wide web across a yellow rose bush. [PAUSE] I heard a strange gurgling sound, turned, and there he was, standing behind me with his pants around his ankles. [PAUSE] I started backing up into the bush until I felt the thorns in my back, and hair. [PAUSE] He stood there for a minute or two, talking to me in fast words "Hey baby, come to uncle Hermie," words that didn't make sense to my little girl ears. [PAUSE] I started to cry, but before I could open my mouth to scream—he held me there trapped choking on my own spit. [PAUSE] When he finished, he cleaned my face with his handkerchief, all the while talking quietly. Told me he knew what I did in my room alone, that liking girls was wrong—that he'd done this to help me understand. [PAUSE] Weird thing is I was more afraid of my parents finding out what Uncle Herman knew than I was determined to tell them what he did to me. [PAUSE] So I said nothing. Uncle Herman moved away right after that—the next time I saw him I was a teenager. [PAUSE] Kept my distance, so did he.

Practicing to kill myself used to be a game. Instead of a styrofoam cup, I waited until no one was home and used our bathtub. I'd get a picture of my latest dream-girlfriend—I was so shy back then, I'd have these gigantic crushes, you know, can't eat, can't sleep, every time I'd run into Judy or Jamie, or Madeline, depending on what grade I was in, I'd stare at them passionately, want to leap tall buildings with a single bound—or at least carry their books for the rest of their lives. [PAUSE] But I was so afraid of what people would think, I'd never say a word, just went home, imagined what it would be like to touch, to taste, to smell their scent, and cry myself to sleep.[PAUSE] I'd take the picture, stand it on the edge of the bathtub, fill the tub with water, put on Three Dog Night, or Average White Band, and sink down under the water holding my breath. [PAUSE] Course this never worked—all I got was soaking wet, water up my nose, and hard-to-manage hair.

I changed when I met Anne. I was standing in the rain waiting for a bus down-town.When the sky cleared, I looked across the street and there she was walk-ing between a mostly blue rainbow right toward me, smiling.Bold and beautiful, when she got closer she held out her hand and said "Hey baby what's your name?" [PAUSE AS SHE ACTS IT OUT] I just reached out, took her hand, and we walked and talked for hours. [PAUSE] Turns out she was a little older than me, 22 to my 19, had just discovered her sexuality during what wound up as a one-night stand, and she approached me 'cause she "felt" my vibe.[PAUSE] We've been to-gether 5 years, and when she says "hey baby" it's always followed by "I love you." [PAUSE] Last week I took her to my parents' garden (it's taken them a while but they're getting used to her), told her the story of the spiders, Uncle Herman, rain, and learning to love me.

2. Empathy with a Rug Left Behind in a Foreclosed House

'Fortune 500' Character Name: Rug
    A long time ago a witch cast a spell on my afro,
    turned me into a rug. Dark brown and nappy
    like my hair, I was cut into pieces at the wholesale
    store, spread around this city like old bricks on side
    streets in the hood.

    Where my hair went, my mind went too and I've been lying
    under stories that strike like footprints,
    each step a new thought, a new way of seeing a world
    that used to hold all of me.

    Lately, this 9x12 patch has held most of my attention.
    I'm the carpet in what used to be a crackhouse, the sound

of Star Trek from the owner's mouth: Beam me up Scotty,
Beam me up Scotty, Beam me up, Ahhhhhhh! Hey, don't let
it go yet—here let me show you—

Violence. Sucka punch, head bang, silence. Smoke.
Worse thing you can do is take a pipe from a head
not ready to let go, who hasn't gotten that feeling
every crackhead worth a rock is searching for—a feeling
I heard a young girl gasp was better than coming, the ride
on the Enterprise that's really a crawl, belly down
in slow motion.

When the lost house was shut down, they put wood
over the doors and windows, but every night someone
with a rock and nowhere to go found a way
to break inside and sit on me for a ride—until word
got around cops were watching.

There's so many tiny, tiny rocks in my head it looks like lint,
and the penny someone left heads up—won't be spent
in this house.

3. Empathy with Death. Coming Full Circle in 2011. Back to the Subject of "Death": My First Poem at Age 13

"Haiku"
> Day. Time for last breath
> too late to leave an I.O.U. for
> what you were to do.

I began using performance-based midterms in the fall of 1996. I'd completed my Master's in English that spring, and after using an all-essay exam for the midterm during an English Composition course I taught that summer, I was dissatisfied with the results, because several students did so poorly. But as I thought about it more deeply, including questioning whether or not there was any long-term benefit all of the exams I'd taken in my educative career, I decided to try something different. Based upon the impact stepping off the page as a poet had on my self-esteem and public speaking ability, I decided to try oral performance.

My fall semester students learned on the first day of class that the only "exam" for the semester required them to (1) pose a pertinent question; (2) address the question in a detailed, well-written response, making certain the answer was between 5 and 7 minutes in length; (3) memorize it using my tips; and (4) using my tips on performance, recite and/or perform the timed midterm in front of their peers without notes of any kind for 25% of their course grade. I decided to make time a requirement because, as I shared with the students, I didn't want anyone to wait until the last minute to get started. For this reason, students also lose 1% of the total for every 30 seconds over or under time.

The first results in 1996 were powerful. Not only did most students pose important questions, their midterms responded to the questions, and for the most part met the time constraint. Further, when I asked them what the difference was between this form of assessment and an all-essay or multiple choice exam, each "student" without exception (this response has been consistent each year) stated that this was much more difficult. Many commented they learned not only from their own midterm but from the variety of presentations shared by their peers, and—unlike with written exams they'd taken—they will remember this experience.

All of this came as a surprise to me, because since I'd never tried this before, I had no assumptions or expectations, but I knew I'd never give another traditional exam. For the next 10 years, including during my tenure as a doctoral student, I used this form of assessment as described above in both the English and Education classes I was hired to teach as an adjunct faculty member. In the fall of 2008, I became a full-time faculty member in a Department of Education. I was hired to teach courses in multicultural education, including the Foundations of Education. I started thinking about the need for the current and future teachers in my classes to more closely identify with their students, especially students from different racial, ethnic, class, religious, and sexual-orientation backgrounds. I revised the midterm guidelines to require students to empathize with an experience outside of their own.

At first I restricted the midterm subjects to the above-noted areas, but over the years students have asked if they could empathize with deaf culture, attention deficit disorder (ADD), autism, poverty, sexual assault, intersexuality, alcoholism, cancer, and bullying, to name a few. I have videotaped many of the midterms for my archives and to share with colleagues interested in trying this form of assessment. In 2010, I started offering students the opportunity to view examples of past midterms without sharing the grade that selected students earned. At the request of my department, I also started using a formal rubric to grade them.

Each semester I look forward to what a new class of students will come up with. I'm never bored with this process, and I'm usually surprised and moved, sometimes to tears, by the results. Several midterms have stayed with me over the years. In one a young, white female became a tree in an Indian village before the whites came. The student described what it was like the first time the village was attacked and ended by becoming the bench where the Indians came to cry. In another, a young African American male empathized with a young, immigrant mother working in a sweatshop. He used a slideshow of images of sweatshops as a backdrop while "Ave Maria" played in the background. Last semester a biracial graduate student did her midterm as a female, homeless veteran.

These midterms have become the centerpiece of my education classes. All learning is reciprocal, and each semester I learn more about my students during this process. After each performance we come closer together as a learning community. According to my students, this is because they discover so much about their peers through this process, and they all go through it together. At the end of each semester I ask students to write a final essay on the most important experiences they'll take from our class. The overwhelming majority reference the midterm experience. This is a sampling of comments from the final essays of students in my fall 2011 classes:

> I was amazed at the immense diversity of the presentations and how well each student did in empathizing with this character they had created and studied. Again, like the Takaki reading, this experience was a huge eye opener and an experience…I will cherish forever.
> I was happy that this class was so much more than learning stereotypes about cultures in order to make someone feel comfortable in a classroom. It would be a lie to say that a specific strategy will work for any person of a specific race. Instead, I was much happier that this class demonstrated how to develop empathy for students, and it's that empathy that will allow for understanding and acceptance.
> The role-playing project that we did was particularly helpful in allowing me to think different. I suppose that I never considered how difficult…it is to be a homosexual in today's society, particularly in an all boys' Jesuit high school. I realized that my high school was a hostile environment towards homosexuals at times. I was able to empathize with homosexuals through my role-playing…. I found myself feeling personally attacked as I recited my speech.

What follows is the work of three former students: Valerie Leonard, graduate student, and undergraduates Odell Brown and Andrea Frabotta. The work is published with their permission:

Crawling into the Skin of Another: A Multidimensional Assessment
Valerie Leonard, Graduate Student

Authentic assessment is a buzzword in education today, but it is rarely modeled in university education classes as effectively as it was in Dr. Weems's class. Truly democratic, the assignment gave students creative freedom while maintaining a consistent standard for excellence. This assessment also contributed to the creation of a learning community in the class by encouraging trust, honest feedback, and scaffolding. Not only did we learn from each other's presentations, we learned how to assess such performances by reflecting on the midterms and noting strengths in others' conception or delivery.

While written exams can often gauge understanding, assigning a grade to the final product is complicated by the quality of the writing, a strong point for some students but not others. Since this was not a writing class, this form of assessment allowed us to demonstrate our particular strengths while still incorporating what was learned from material and class discussion. There was certainly writing involved, but Dr. Weems was not grading the written portion, which motivated students whose writing skills were not their strong points.

All components of the Imagination-Intellect Theory were evident in this assignment. The opportunity for aesthetic appreciation was present in observing and reflecting on others' performances, an element many found to be the most enjoyable. Written expression worked hand in hand with oral expression in the composition and delivery of the performance, whether it was a monologue, a poem, or "other." Dramatic performance was probably the most intimidating and challenging for most members of the class—and the greatest surprise, as many (including myself!) found they were more skilled and confident than they had imagined. But perhaps the most profound learning was in the area of social consciousness. Because of the emphasis on empathy and authenticity, the performances were stirring and memorable.

Not only did we crawl into another's psyche for our own performance, we did so through the performances of others, and it was a memorable experience. A lot of great conversation and deep critical thinking followed, in which many expressed that they'd be able to empathize at a higher level with those from other cultures or those struggling today to be fully accepted. My midterm (the written portion) was startling to compose. I began to empathize with the very real character I created when I sat down, pen in hand, to answer the question I posed:

What was it like for a young, Jewish woman who worked in the garment industry and perished in the Triangle Shirtwaist Company fire?

> *They said that we hit the pavement like hail, but hail does not know fear. Or courage. Before the fire we told them it was not safe. Twenty thousand workers rose up and demanded safer conditions, but we were arrested and beaten. Now, our mothers are tearing their hair and screaming for their daughters.*

> *You who wear clothing with tiny, even stitches: whose hands have clothed you? Do you think of those hands now?*

You who sit behind the desk and count the money: whose sweat, whose aching shoulders have fed you? Do you ever see our faces in your sleep?

I loved to dance. Did you know that? My body came alive at night—my hips swaying under my skirt. There was a boy with dark eyes whose hands were warm, and he danced with me until the sky was pink with morning. I was only brave with him while we were dancing.

How the building burned. The flies who had always troubled us escaped, but we could not. Every doorway was made of fire. Have you ever seen a flame decide on you? It appears, tonguing the wall, creeping closer, and suddenly—it sees you. It reaches for you, encircles you, no matter how small you try to make yourself, and you are swallowed in its embrace.

There was no thought in the monotonous work, only repetition, the droning of the machines, the heat, the flies…and sometimes, the needles piercing our bones. When evening came, the air of the city was as cool and clean as water. Our lungs were grateful. We streamed from the tenements, out into the street, and gathered in Jackson Street Park. There was music and laughter, and the children played joyously. One summer evening, I sat on a bench and stole shy glances at the dark-eyed boy who was my dance partner. I imagined that someday, one of the laughing children would be ours.

I never saw my wedding day. Fifty thousand poured into the streets to march in our memory. My mother didn't march. She stayed in her room, drew the shades, and climbed into bed. She neither ate nor slept, merely stared blankly into the darkness. My best friend remembered me well, but she did not march, either, because she was half-mad, having herself worked at the factory and barely escaped, jumping from the second-story window. She hurt her leg, and it would heal, but her mind and heart were beyond repair.

Some of the ones who jumped would survive; others would not. I never had the chance, seated as I was at the end of a row, away from the windows. The confusion and the screaming…I cannot describe it. All I wanted was air, but the flames stole the oxygen and replaced it with smoke, thick and blinding.

Once during a dance, the dark-eyed boy paused and caught my eyes with his. I felt as if I couldn't breathe, and as if I had no need to. We continued to sway to the music as we kissed, and it was perfect. I live in that moment eternally. My fingers and my hands are at rest, settled lightly on his shoulders, and the flies do not disturb us here.

The impact this assignment has had on me—personally and professionally—cannot be overstated. As a "non-traditional" student returning to college after a 15-year hiatus, I found that I was nervous and withdrawn in public speaking situations. After speaking with Dr. Weems, I found her suggestion that I dim the lights and have a candle for my performance helpful.... [A]s an education student, I see the possibilities for this type of assessment not only for people struggling with nervousness, but also for students with special needs.... The proliferation of authentic talent among all students should be considered the most valuable resource in education, and it costs absolutely nothing.

Not the Smurfs
Odell Brown, Sophomore

What is it like to be a gay male in America?

What follows is the text of the midterm I culled from the interviews, memorized, and presented in our class within the required time limit of 5–7 minutes:

I don't want to waste much time so I'll come right out and say it, I'm gay. If you are thinking to yourself well gee, you don't look gay then you have the wrong idea about what gay men look like. We're not all flamboyant, with high voices, wearing tight clothes, and have feminine gestures. That is an extremely annoying stereotype. Gay men are still men, and we are masculine men. For some reason as soon as I get comfortable with people they always ask when did I turn homosexual? It'd be like me asking you when did you turn heterosexual? As far as I can remember I've been this way, although I can remember one of my earliest sexual experiences. It's not the easiest thing in the world to talk about but....I was 5 years old and my father left some tape around the house; I thought it would be power rangers, or the Smurfs or some type of cartoon. Then I put it in and saw something that looked like a sock, smacking into something that I had never seen before. I was watching porn. I wasn't even nervous because I didn't even know what it was. I'm not sure about everything that happened psychologically when I watched that tape but right after I finished watching the tape I ran into my cousin who was the same age and I asked him "Do you want to Frankie?" Frankie was a term we used to talk about sex. My cousin and I didn't really know what we needed to do to Frankie but we did kiss, and I liked it. At that moment I became more attracted to males in a physical sense. I enjoyed that experience and I wanted more of it.

I guess it was around 2nd grade I saw guys as being attractive yet I didn't even know what gay was. Others didn't practice it so I didn't practice it. Growing up I can remember being infatuated with Zena the princess warrior. I would watch it religiously with my mother, and I would go around the house imitating Zena and my mother did not think anything of it. In fact all the way up until high school it was like I couldn't do a thing wrong. My mother was ok with whatever I was into. Now that I look back at it my mom had to notice some signs of me being gay. She knew that I never had a girlfriend, and I never really talked about girls, and I was not really that into sports; and my heroes were Zena and Sandra Bullock. My mom never questioned me, at all. She never approached me and asked was I this, or did I do that. It's almost like she was totally oblivious to the possibility of being gay. It wasn't until high school that she gained suspicions of me being gay. There was this activity I had to do in my homeroom class on Valentine's Day, we had to draw names out of a hat and write a letter of appreciation to that person. My best friend who was a guy coincidentally drew my name so he had to write me a letter, and nobody thought it was gay or anything and since we were already friends he had genuine things to say. I put the letter in my room and it got lost somewhere. Then my mother found it and asked me about it later. She knew the two of us spent a lot of time with each other, and in a hopeless voice she asked me if he was my boyfriend. I told her no he was not and explained the school assignment to her. That was the end of that situation but periodically my mom would mention bible scriptures that condemned homosexuality, scriptures in Leviticus. I don't remember all the specifics but basically homosexuals burn in hell was what I got out of it. Then for the first time she asked me if I was gay. I knew she could not handle it at the time, so I lied and said no. Eventually I got sick and tired of being sick and tired with all the pretending to be something that I was not. I can still remember the day I decided to tell my parents I was gay, it was June 19, 2007. I was actually studying dance at UCLA so I was away from home. I decided to tell my dad first. I called him and just said it "Dad I'm gay." He asked me a lot of questions about it but the main message was that he loved me no matter what. My father and I actually grew closer together because of this incident. Telling my mom I was gay was a lot tougher. It's like my soul was on fire when I uttered the words to her. She did not get all ballistic or crazy like I thought she would. She just told me in a very pleasant voice that I needed to see a shrink, and that was literally it. She never even called the next day to talk about the situation or anything. Even when I returned back home we never had a big conversation about my sexuality. She would mention it here and there but mostly I felt like she wanted to suppress it, or ignore it. I waited until senior year of high school to tell any of my friends I was gay. It was the worst decision of my life. My community of friends changed almost instantly, even my best friend that I mentioned earlier stopped talking to me because he did not want people to think he was gay. Absolutely everybody assumed I was having sex a lot. And my classmates treated me like I had aids, or some type of deadly disease. Whenever I looked at a guy he would assume that I was attracted to him or wanted to have sex with him. It's not like every girl that a straight guy sees he wants to have sex with. Of all classes gym was probably the most uncomfortable to me. I was really intimidated by the other guys in the gym because I didn't want them to feel like I was checking them out. I eventually just trained myself to not look men in the eye. I don't think a day went by without me being called a fag. It was like my sexual orientation was the only thing people saw when they looked at me. When I graduated high school I was relieved. The gay-bashing was over. I thought that the university would be a place where I could be openly and comfortably gay. I am a spiritual person so I wanted a religious education. The Jesuits are known for seeing God in everything so they could certainly see God in me. I made my sexual orientation on Facebook official and I enrolled at the university. My first experience in college just like every other student was my new student orientation session. I had a lot of fun with the dance off, and diversity exercises, and just meeting all the new people. Everything was fresh, new. I can remember meeting my roommate for the first time. He was going into the ROTC and I wanted to be a language major and was considering ROTC. He seemed like a nice enough guy so I felt comfortable telling him that I was a little worried about joining ROTC because I am gay and I don't know how people will react. He looked devastated when I told him this and he requested a new roommate. Once the school year started I met a lot of good people, but there was still a few ignorant people too. The first week of school people would pound on my door shouting faggot while running away. I also saw comments about me written in bathroom stalls, and someone changed my nametag to say "Queer" instead of my name. Most of the discrimination is indirect. But it still hurts. My family, my friends, and society at large all make it seem like there is something wrong with me, like my very existence is inadequate, or immoral. I'm tired of all the homophobia, and gay-bashing, and discrimination I have received because of my sexual orientation, it has really made school and life hard for me. I am just a man looking to love and to be loved.

The abundance of good information I gained through interviewing the five people has caused me to see homosexuals as humans, different only in sexual orientation. The imaginings of my intellect are now more informed. I can imagine having a friend who is homosexual, and my intellect can now control my imagination so that unfounded fears no longer cause me to make irrational choices.

Experiencing Empathy in the Eye of Another
Andrea M. Frabotta, Junior

In preparation for the midterm, I chose to become a metaphorical character, Rashida Sahar. I immersed myself in the character of Rashida, a 38-year-old Afghanistan-American immigrant who came to the United States to escape the persecution of the Taliban…. I…conducted research…[that] involved delving into interviews, history textbooks, and video recordings.

What is like to be an Afghanistan immigrant in America?

My name is Rashida Sahar. I am 38 years old and I am an Afghan-American woman. I wear a chadri and burqa, which I will explain to you. As I would like to connect with you and really see you when I talk to you, I will remove my chadri. I am only removing this because I trust you. I will explain my feelings to you as I tell you why I came to this country.

I have a strong sense of family. We are very close knit and have been through very difficult times together. I am loyal to my father, mother, and two older brothers. I did not come here by choice, but by necessity. I fled the terrible warfare in Afghanistan. It was no longer safe to live there because of the constant attacks and the strict rule of the Taliban. My father immigrated to the United States in 1999. He was lucky enough to obtain a visa. He needed to live in the United States for a few years before bringing my mother, brothers and me over. To obtain visas for us, my father needed to prove that he could support us when we arrived. Because my father had education as a medical doctor, he began a practice with an American doctor in the United States. Luckily that American doctor helped my father learn the English language. We are forever grateful to this man.

Before we immigrated the conditions in Afghanistan were atrocious. In 1995, just before the Taliban took power, I had graduated from the University of Kabul to become a school teacher. When the Taliban took control just one year later in 1996, every right I ever had was stripped away. I was banished from teaching, my passion. I also was prohibited from leaving my home unless I was with my brother or father. If I did leave my home, I was required to wear this burqa and chadri.

I'll never forget the first time that I wore the burqa and chadri. I felt so isolated and suffocated. I could barely see where I was walking. I tripped several times. I remember not being able to recognize any of my female friends. We all looked the same…we had to learn to recognize one another by our body movements. In Afghanistan the climate is extremely warm and dry. I was so overheated from wearing the thick fabric of the burqa that I fainted in the market. I suffered from heat exhaustion. It took a while to get used to wearing this burqa. The consequences of not wearing the burqa or wearing it incorrectly were much more severe than heat exhaustion. My brother's wife and I were in the market and the fabric of her burqa got caught on the edge of a basket exposing a small part of her skin. Members of the Taliban spotted her and beat her with cables for ten minutes straight. No one could stop it. I was so frightened that I would be next. I cried out of heartbreak for my dear sister-in-law.

There is one day in your history and mine that will never be forgotten. That day was September 11, 2001. It changed the lives of Americans as well as those from the Middle East. Just as the American people felt the sadness of violence and loss that day, I can truly understand your feelings, because I lived through the same violence and loss in Afghanistan every day. Bombings and gunfire were a typical daily presence that we had to avoid. It was the reason I came here to America. So when the Taliban intruded on your country, those of us from the Middle East were scared that they were following us here. The last thing in the world that I ever wanted was to be associated with the Taliban. They are an extremist reform group. They are not a positive reflection of typical citizens of Afghanistan. Not everyone in the Middle East acts as they do, with hatred and violence. Unfortunately the media has forced you to think that way. After September 11th, Americans became skeptical of me and my family because of our descent. I had one American come up to me and ask, "Do you have a bomb under that burqa?" This has made me feel ashamed to be who I am. Every time I go to an airport or event with security, my sister in law and I are always targeted, simply because of the way we look. I am an innocent and have nothing to hide, but I am filled with great sadness for the way I am judged.

I do not want your pity for my struggles. It is these experiences that have made me the strong woman I am today. But if there is one thing I ask of you.… Please do not judge someone before you know them. Don't have hate in your heart. The Taliban based their horrific actions on ignorance. Learn for yourself; be open to others. I think of that wonderful doctor who helped my father. We need more people and acceptance like this in our world.

But, even now as we live in the United States away from the violence, we still wear our burqas out of fear. Fear of the violence and aggression exerted towards us. It became so natural to us, that we feel uncomfortable without it. Perhaps it is hiding the woman inside, but now I want to end that fearful chapter of my life. As I have finally spoken my story, I will remove my burqa forever more and let my true colors shine.

Each of the students' work embodies the imagination-intellect theory in practice. All of the examples speak to the significance of the theory and how it can move us closer to a world of one love through the educative experience in any classroom.

I selected the following chapters for this book because they represent authors with astute imagination-intellects, and a commitment to pursuing a more just, inclusive society. Their writings both resist injustice and offer the possibility of beginning the healing process for themselves and all who engage this work.

> I celebrate teaching that enables transgressions—a movement against and beyond boundaries. It is that movement which makes education the practice of freedom.
> —bell hooks (1994, p. 12)

References

Ang, R.P., & Goh, D.H. (2010).Cyberbullying among adolescents: The role of affective and cognitive empathy, and gender. *Child Psychology Human Development,41*, 387–397.

Barr, J.J., & Higgins-D'Alessandro. A. (2009). How adolescent empathy and prosocial behavior changes in the context of school culture: A two-year longitudinal study. *Adolescence, 44*(176),751–772.

Batson, C.D., Chang, J., Orr, R., & Rowland, J. (2002). Empathy, attitudes, and action: Can feeling for a member of a stigmatized group motivate one to help the group? *Personality and Social Psychology Bulletin, 28*(12), 1656–1666.

Brooks, S. (2009). Historical empathy in the social studies classroom: A review of the literature. *The Journal of Social Studies Research, 33*(2), 213–234.

Caravita, S.C.S., & Di Blasio, P. (2009). Unique and interactive effects of empathy and social status on involvement in bullying. *Social Development, 18*(1), 139–163.

Carse, A.L. (2005). The moral contours of empathy. *Ethical Theory and Moral Practice, 8*(1/2), 169–195.

Chiao, J.Y., &Mathur, V.A. (2010). Intergroup empathy: How does race affect empathic neural responses? *Current Biology, 20*(11), 478–479.

Cooper, B. (2010). In search of profound empathy in learning relationships: Understanding the mathematics of moral learning environments. *Journal ofMoral Education, 39*(1), 79–99.

Cunningham, D. (2009). An empirical framework for understanding how teachers conceptualize and cultivate historical empathy in students. *Journal of Curriculum Studies, 41*(5), 679–709.

Exline, J.J., & Zell, A.L. (2009). Empathy, self-affirmation, and forgiveness: The moderating roles of gender and entitlement. *Journal of Social and Clinical Psychology, 28*(9), 1071–1099.

Gerdes, K.E., & Segal, E.A. (2011). The importance of empathy for social work practice: Integrating new science. *Social Work, 56*(2), 141–148.

Gladstein, G.A. (1983). Understanding empathy: Integrating counseling, developmental, and social psychology perspectives. *Journal of Counseling Psychology, 30*(4), 467–482.

Gorrell, N. (2000). Teaching empathy through ecphrastic poetry: Entering a curriculumof peace. *The English Journal, 89*(5), 32–41.

Greene, M. (1995). *Releasing the imagination*. San Francisco, CA: Jossey-Bass.

Hojat, M. (2009).Ten approaches for enhancing empathy in health and human services cultures. *Journal of Health and Human Services Administration, 31*(4), 412–450.

Hollan, D., & Throop, C.J. (2008). Whatever happened to empathy? Introduction. *Ethos, 36*(4) 385–401.

hooks, b. (1994).*Teaching to transgress: Education as the practice of freedom*. New York: Routledge.

Knight, P. (1989). Empathy: Concept, confusion and consequences in a national curriculum. *Oxford Review of Education, 15*(1), 41–53.

Lane, R.E. (2001). Self-reliance and empathy: The enemies of poverty: And of the poor. *Political Psychology, 22*(3), 473–492.

Lindquist, J. (2004). Class affectations: Working through the paradoxes of strategic empathy. *College English, 67*(2), 187–209.

Loggia, M.L., Mogil, J.S., & Bushnell, M.C. (2008). Empathy hurts: Compassion for another increases both sensory and affective components of pain perception. *International Association for the Study of Pain, 136*, 168–176.

Lu, Y.E., Dane, B., & Gellman, A. (2005). An experimental model: Teaching empathy and cultural sensitivity. *Journal of Teaching in Social Work, 25*(3/4), 89–103.

Maxwell, B., & DesRoches, S. (2010). Empathy and social-emotional learning: Pitfalls and touchstones for school-based programs. *New Directions for Child and Adolescent Development, 129*, 33–53.

Meek, C. (1957). An experiment in teaching empathy. *Journal of Educational* Sociology, *31*(2), 107–110.

Moore, R.J., & Hallenbeck, J. (2010). Narrative empathy and how dealing with stories helps: Creating a space for empathy in culturally diverse care settings. *Journal of Pain and Symptom Management, 40*(3), 471–476.

Morgan, H., & York, K.C. (2009). Examining multiple perspectives with creative think-alouds. *The Reading Teacher, 63*(4), 307–311.

Panosky, D., & Diaz, D. (2009).Teaching caring and empathy through simulation. *International Journal for Human Caring, 13*(3), 44–46.

Parks, G. (1986). *A choice of weapons.* St. Paul: Minnesota Historical Society Press.

Perry, T., Steele, C., & Hilliard, A., III (Eds.). (2003). *To be young, gifted and black: Promoting high achievement among African-American students.* Boston: Beacon Press.

Rangganadhan, A., & Todorov, N. (2010). Personality and self-forgiveness: The roles of shame, guilt, empathy and conciliatory behavior. *Journal of Social and Clinical Psychology, 29*(1), 1–22.

Rasoal, C., Jungert, T., Hau, S., Stiwne, E.E., & Anderson, G. (2009).Ethnocultural empathy among students in health care education. *Evaluation and the Health Professions, 32*(3), 300–313.

Rumble, A.C., Van Lange, P.A.M., & Parks, C.D. (2010). The benefits of empathy: When empathy may sustain cooperation in social dilemmas. *European Journal of Social Psychology, 40*, 856–866.

Sams, D.P., & Truscott, S.D. (2004). Empathy, exposure to community violence, and use of violence among urban, at-risk adolescents. *Child & Youth Care Forum, 33*(1), 33–50.

Schwebel, M. (2006). Realistic empathy and active nonviolence confront political reality. *Journal of Social Issues, 62*(1), 191–208.

Vygotsky, L.S. (1978). *Mind in society.* London and Cambridge, MA: Harvard University Press.

Vygotsky, L.S. (1986). *Thought and Language* (Alex Kozulin, Trans.) Cambridge, MA: MIT Press.

Weems, M.E. (2003). *Public education and the imagination intellect: I speak from the wound in my mouth.* New York: Peter Lang.

Weems, M.E. (2009a). Food for thought: The imagination-intellect and the role of empathy. *Iowa Journal of Communications, 41*(1), 149–161.

Weems, M.E. (2009b). The E in poetry stands for empathy. In M. Prendergast, C. Leggo, & P. Sameshima, (Eds.), *Poetic inquiry: Vibrant voices in the social sciences* (pp. 133–144). Boston: Sense Publishers.

two

A Space for Imagination
The Power of Group Process and Reflective Writing to Cultivate Empathy for Self and Others

Susan V. Iverson

In a global society with rapidly changing demographics, educators are called to engage with diverse groups and support the educational achievement of individuals from varied backgrounds. To respond to this call, faculty in professional preparation programs design curriculum to develop the multicultural competence of their students (Pope, Reynolds, & Mueller, 2004), inclusive of *awareness* (of self and the impact it has on others), *knowledge* (of diverse cultures and groups), and *skills* (ability to openly discuss differences). Yet, in my efforts to facilitate the development of these competencies with my students, I have been left with questions: How might the development of multicultural competencies serve to maintain the status quo more than inspire creative thinking about the root of social problems? In what ways might our (taken-for-granted) assumptions about the "goodness" of multicultural competence leave us falling short in enacting a commitment to social justice or critical consciousness? As an instructor of a required graduate-level course on diversity in higher education, I challenge students to ask questions about taken-for-granted assumptions in our field of higher education administration in an effort to develop multicultural competence informed by a critical stance.

Toward this end, I strive to design spaces for students to exercise their voice and agency. However, I wrestle with the aesthetic distance students maintain in their academic pursuits: they gaze at the "object" under study, unaware that each of us is part of and can be found in that which we study. Guided by Weems's (2003)

articulation of the relationship between intellect and imagination, I structured my
graduate-level diversity course with an emphasis on self-awareness. More specifically, I incorporated small-group dialogue to cultivate self-awareness and empathy
for others and assigned reflective writing to help students make sense and meaning of their educational experiences. Drawing upon students' reflective writing,
I share in this chapter the ways in which some students did, and others did not,
develop greater social consciousness. Further, I offer possibilities for future teaching: how we might form a script of the drama of their experiences to offer a space
for students to imagine their (un)negotiated performances of identity.

Conceptual Context for Course: Privilege and Discrimination

In the required graduate seminar on diversity in higher education that I teach, students are introduced "to theories, concepts, policies, controversies, challenges and
possibilities related to gender, racial, ethnic, sexual orientation, socio-economic,
ability, and religious differences among students, faculty, administrators, and
other employees in postsecondary settings" (excerpted from syllabus). Through
my teaching, I expose students to oppressive structures that are often invisible to
those who occupy privileged groups. I assign two particular readings to serve as
conceptual scaffolding for our thinking and discussion. Johnson's *Privilege, Power
and Difference* (2006) introduces students to the concept of privilege. Building
on Peggy McIntosh's essay on white privilege, Johnson introduces the reader to
the social construction of difference and how the world is "organized in ways that
encourage people to *use* difference to include or exclude, reward or punish, credit
or discredit, elevate or oppress, value or devalue, leave alone or harass" (p. 16,
italics in original). Johnson further challenges the reader to use the words he asserts we have abandoned and to initiate conversations about the problem: racism,
patriarchy, privilege, and oppression.

In my course, students also read the essay "The Problem: Discrimination,"
which distinguishes individual oppression from organizational and structural oppression (U.S. Commission on Civil Rights, 1981/2001). White students in my
class, if they acknowledge racism at all, generally perceive incidents of discrimination as isolated acts committed by a biased, bigoted individual; rarely are they
aware of structural oppression. So, as they cautiously consider these concepts, students, noting this essay's publication date, too quickly dismiss organizational and
structural discrimination as "a thing of the past." To further illustrate these concepts and make visible the social, economic, and political conditions that dispro-
portionately channel advantages to white people, I show episode 3, "The House
We Live In," of the 3-part documentary *Race: The Power of an Illusion* (Smith,
2003). This segment powerfully describes the ways in which U.S. institutions and
policies advantage some groups at the expense of others. For many students, this

is a turning point in our conversations. We have the potential (albeit not always realized) to have richer discussions about not only race in society, but other forms of oppression along multiple dimensions of identity, e.g., gender, sexuality, and religion. Students slowly begin to identify policies and practices in their everyday lives that provide further evidence of institutionalized discrimination. And from here I invite students to imagine alternative ways of organizing and being in the world.

Facilitating Self-Awareness

My facilitation of their thinking about these ideas—privilege and structural discrimination—also requires their *un*thinking of dominant narratives. My students, who are predominantly white, have limited experience living and working with people unlike themselves. Questions of gender, sexuality, race, ethnicity, and socioeconomic status tend to fall on the deaf ears of students who grew up and were schooled in fairly homogeneous environments. In discussions about difference and inequality, too often students will assert that all people have equal opportunity, and "hard work" is necessary to rise and meet life's challenges; that they survived, even succeeded, in school, so too can others achieve if they work hard and have "good" parental support. And, as we begin to name race, they assert that they don't see color. The need, then, to help students become more self-aware emerged as pivotal, for if these students remain unaware of their assumptions and biases, they will forever be contributing, perhaps unwittingly, to the problems we wish so much to address in education. Without self-awareness, students might gather their multicultural knowledge and skills like tools in a toolbox that they could pull out when they need to "repair" a social problem. So through my course I sought ways to draw out from students how they really feel; ways to engage in the self-reflexive work through which individuals (might) unpack their identities, reveal their blind spots, and interrogate the given-ness of what they know.

I have assigned to students self-reflective exercises such as the autobiographical essay, so they can engage in self-examination as a means of achieving greater consciousness of the spaces we inhabit and our relation to others so that we might act more justly in the world. Yet I am also aware of the limitations of such strategies. While some students will engage in critical self-examination, far more complete the autobiographical essay as nothing more than a transaction for a grade and fail to critically and deeply explore themselves or to consider how (newfound) understandings might (could) influence personal choices, professional actions, and the ways one views and interacts with others (James, 2008).

Recognizing the power and potential for others to hold a mirror to one's evolving understanding of self, I turned to the possibility of facilitated dialogue groups, coupled with individual reflective writing, as a means of cultivating self-awareness—as an invitation for students to ask questions, to take risks, to imagine and "envision alternative realities" (Weems, 2003, p. 7). Weems describes this as "imagination-intellectual development," and I wanted to cultivate "an increasingly imagination-intellectually astute student population well-equipped to love the pursuit of knowledge, to question, to criticize, to affect positive social change" (p. 3). Further, the power of empathy—seen in and through the eyes of others—can be felt through group storytelling about self and others, and can play a crucial role in developing social and self-consciousness. Weems identifies "social consciousness" as one of five areas at the core of imagination-intellectual development. Students, she argues, need to gain

> an awareness of their social position in society enabling them to honor diversity, and to put social justice including the importance of a true participatory democracy at the forefront. A creative-critical, social consciousness shapes an imagination-intellect capable of envisioning, and actively working toward a better, more humane world. (Weems, 2003, pp. 5–6)

In my class, students meet once each week for nearly 3 hours, and in addition to interactive engagement with assigned readings, they view films and listen to music to facilitate our (un)thinking about diversity in higher education. Students also participate in small group dialogue sessions. Six 60–90 minute sessions are held during class time; students disperse to designated rooms, and each group is co-facilitated by two graduate students in the educational counseling program. I do not attend, and I am not privy to the content of their sessions.

Students are also given the assignment of maintaining a reflective journal, with one entry per week. While most entries are student initiated (I provide no writing prompt), four of their entries are guided. These include: (1) an initial entry prepared as a letter to oneself, articulating challenges, feelings, discomfort related to diversity; (2) a self-awareness essay through which students reflect on individual identity and social group memberships; (3) a mid-semester reflection; and (4) a final reflective entry for which students must re-read all their journal entries and offer a reply to their initial "letter to self." Further, regarding this reflective journal, students are told that it is not an archive of what they read or did in the semester, but it is

> a space in which to narrate one's growing sense of self; a place to imagine from where one came and to where one might go; an emerging script of one's life, as it has been lived and will or might be lived; a safety net for fears turned away from and to which one later hopes to return; a "high wire" for taking risks in relation to one's own intellectual and socio-political position; a creative corner for intellectual play and to "craft" yourself. (excerpted from syllabus)

The reflective journal invites one to "see anew in ways that are not totally saturated with the known" (Gitlin, 2005, p. 17). My hope is that this might cultivate what Weems (2003) refers to as the imagination-intellect: aesthetic, interpretive, and experiential processes of knowing.

Reflecting on Experience

In this section I share the ways in which some students did, and others did not, develop greater social consciousness. As a reminder, I was not privy to their dialogue in the group session, except if and when they described moments from their sessions in their reflective journals, which they did often. So here I weave together excerpts from their reflective journals to "narrate" their evolving understanding of their selves, the dissonance of their experiences, and their (un)negotiated dimensions of identity.

The aim was for students to intersect their growing knowledge of course concepts with interactive experiences in group dialogue sessions, and to imagine, through their reflective journaling, the stories of and possibilities for their growing self-awareness. Evident in their writing is their struggle to find and use their voices. Students wrote in their journals about their frustration, surprise, dismay, interest, and anger at another person's actions or words, but also confessed to an inability to articulate their thoughts, feelings, concerns, and (counter) viewpoints when face-to-face with their peers.

Difficult Dialogues

Many students wrote in their journals that the group dialogue sessions were valuable, as Judy[1] stated, for "finding out what others think and hearing their insight." Some students realized a shared experience with others. For instance, Julia observed, "During the group counseling discussion, some of the people in class who were first generation mentioned their individual stories. It was interesting to hear that my own experience was somewhat close to their stories." However, when viewpoints diverged, students shared their discomfort—and often their subsequent silence. Julia, the first-generation, low-income student, wrote in her journal that

> one classmate mentioned [in group session] that some students aren't meant to go to college. Another said that there are jobs that need to be filled, and they aren't for the college educated. It made me feel really weird to hear that.... I know that some people aren't cut out for academics, but that shouldn't be an excuse for high schools to not prepare all students for college. Probably trade schools help some low income students, but...I hate the idea that just because you are low income or are first generation, you are expected not to go away to a four year college.

This muted engagement was pronounced in students' reflections following one group session in which one student shared a local news story about high school students chanting anti-gay slurs at football players wearing light blue uniforms. Noting in his journal that several of his peers felt the administrative response was "too lax," Jake found "most disturbing" that his classmates were quick to dismiss the notion that the students' chants were anti-gay. He wrote that his peers argued that "people were just too sensitive when it came to the issues of name calling and labels attached to groups. The consensus [by his peers in the group dialogue] was that no matter what word was used to describe a group of people, the word could eventually have a negative meaning attached to it and could be a never ending process." Julia added, "I felt like the outsider during the discussion [when I said] that all of those students who were chanting should be suspended.... I think that these students need to be made an example that language and action like that will not be tolerated." Reflecting on "what we didn't talk about," Jake wondered: "It may be because these words have been used against a certain group of individuals constantly throughout their lives and, for that group, these labeling words have a negative connotation. Since the privileged group has never felt the power of the word, they may take the stance that individuals are just overly sensitive to these words." Alice, too, observed that "many of my classmates in the group process seem to believe that race and discrimination issues are not real and that people are too sensitive. They think that the students need to get over things and move on—to toughen up." She added, "I think it is important to be able to tactfully challenge their thought processes and hopefully over time they will start to see another point of view." Yet, typically quiet in class and group dialogue, Alice noted that "no one likes to be the 'bad guy' who puts his/her foot down on an inappropriate comment by a friend or talks to the supervisor about an individual that is not inclusive." In the final week of the semester, Alice reflected, "I must stand up for what I believe in and help others to join me in the fight."

Awareness of Self and Privilege

Others echoed Alice's growing self-awareness. As an example, Julia reflected:

> I think that group process is really starting to make me think about my identity and privilege a lot more, which is helping me in my transformation.... Sometimes it's eye-opening, in a depressing or frustrating way, when people can't understand their own privilege.... It is hard to be completely honest...[and] to put yourself in a vulnerable situation.... Even if I can't open up entirely, thinking critically about my values and ideas are helping me work my way through the issues we are talking about in class.

Similarly, Kim, at the end of the semester, reflected how her understanding of her own racial privilege was developing. The group process, Kim wrote, "has contributed to my overall understanding of me in the context of the world.... I can be an advocate for those who are not as privileged as I am. And why not use privilege to my advantage? I'm white; listen to me…as I tell you why you shouldn't be listening to me just because I'm white!"

For more students, though, opportunities to imagine and think about one's privilege were resisted. Evidence can be found in journal excerpts following a group dialogue session held after the class viewed *Skin Deep*, a documentary film on college students confronting racism (Reid, 1995). In this film, students from different racial, religious, and economic backgrounds attend a 3-day, inter-group dialogue. Most striking to my predominantly white students were the comments made by the white students in the film who are confronted and challenged about their racial privilege. The white students in the film have a powerful awakening, as they have not considered their race prior to this weekend. Many of the white students in my class were empathetic and protective, and even angry. For instance, one student asked in her journal, "How are we, as white individuals, supposed to learn about other minority groups if we attend a program or event and they don't want us there or they make us feel bad for being present" (Marie). Another student, referring to the inter-group conflict in the film, wrote: "It was almost like there was a secret the white kids didn't know about and then everyone unloaded on them. Sometimes I feel that way as well. I had nothing to do with whom I was born to. I have had to work hard to get where I am and I don't feel that anything was handed to me. I have had some real struggles but I worked through them" (Judy).

These points, fueled by the film, emerged in group process as well. One student reflected:

> This week in group process was about to drive me crazy…. I get it—people face hard times and I have a "poor me" story too, but…whatever beliefs we hold, it is important to challenge them and ensure that we have all the facts and all the knowledge. We can solidify our beliefs but also allow ourselves to be transformed. We need to realize it is OKAY to change what you believe. It is OKAY to open your mind to new things. Of course, that is scary, but it is necessary. (Joanne)

This student's frustration is in stark contrast with her classmate Jimmy, who reflected, "While I don't know everything about black history, I think I am an incredibly accepting person. But I wouldn't have participated as much as the others for fear of offending them. I like it when people are happy and that [the inter-group dialogue in the film] would've been a very difficult setting to be in." This student, in his final entry for the semester, expressed that "we spend a lot of time talking about all that is wrong with our society when it comes to diversity issues. I know it isn't the most glamorous topic because there is still a lot of racism and discrimination, but I think we need to look at the positive side…. I wish we could talk about what we are doing right."

Become Uncomfortable

Some students had a greater readiness for dissonance. Julia, for instance, observed, "I need to *become uncomfortable*. It's inevitable. I have to feel bad to be able to see the truth. There is no going around that concept. I still have, and will always have, a lot of trouble feeling uncomfortable or just 'out there.' The idea of feeling something other than my natural equilibrium is *pretty terrifying*" (italics added). Denise echoed this sentiment: "I need to not be afraid to challenge others' thoughts and perspectives.... It is our responsibility to not only challenge our students in their ways of thinking, but also to challenge our colleagues and ourselves." Peter added:

> The group process sessions were valuable in forcing dialogue on issues of diversity. Through talking with my peers, white privilege is no longer a phrase that immediately shifts me into defensive thinking. Listening to my classmates discuss their feelings towards such ideas helped me to evaluate my own thoughts on topics like white privilege or discriminatory attitudes.... Diversity isn't something I am *comfortable* with, in that *diversity* does not relax me or put me at ease; I think I started this course hoping for that familiarity. I think I now value diversity because diversity takes me away from my own paradigm.... I am now at a place where I am willing to evaluate myself, and at a place where I feel willing to act. (italics in original)

Imagination and Action

I feel some optimism that students were able to reflect on who they are and imagine possibilities for how they will act in the world. But they have not—or have only in limited ways—practiced the skills necessary for enacting what they imagine. They have only just begun. Julia best summed it up:

> In class and in group process, we went through so many different topics, so many hard concepts, so many uncomfortable ideas.... I feel like I am so much more aware.... Something clicked, and though I am only just beginning to unpack my privileges.... I think I'm finally on my way.... Things are making sense, but this now opens up a huge can of worms that I hope I can handle. I'm not as idealistic now about my lofty "equality" dreams. Instead I feel like I'm in the trenches, and the dirty work is just beginning.

Reflective processes, through written expression and awakening social consciousness, can elicit curiosity and invite people to be imaginative about themselves. But I am left wondering what might be a next step in developing the skills needed to perform the role of creative-critical, socially conscious self. A possibility is to script difficult dialogues, or what Nieto (1999) calls "dangerous discourses," that invite students to lean into conflict and dissonance. Here I offer a possible performance crafted from a muted group dialogue session that spurred passionate responses in students' journals.

As I am not privy to the group dialogues, this introduction is speculative, based on students' reflective writings. A student in the first group session at the beginning of the semester must've asked, "So, what do people think about the Muslim mosque being built near the world trade center memorial?" A classmate, Sophie, must've replied, "I don't think the Mosque should be built." This apparently fueled a succession of statements affirming the rights of Muslims to build the mosque, which silenced Sophie. The conversation quickly dissipated and segued to some other, more benign topic.

Several students wrote about this group dialogue session in their journals, and Sophie, in particular, was angry: "so angry I was shaking." As I read their individual reflections, and since only I had the balcony view from which to see all their thoughts, I wondered: *What if they had been able to share these views and beliefs with each other?* Here, using some editorial license to thread together passages from each of their journals, I script the dialogue that would've taken place if their words had been said to each other rather than solely in their journals.

The 9-11 Mosque: A Difficult Dialogue

Ray: So, what do people think about the Muslim mosque being built near the world trade center memorial?

Sophie: I don't want that Mosque built.

Paul: Why?

Sophie: Because the Muslim people should not have a place to come together to worship and build a community so close to where their people killed so many.

Ray: Whoa, I didn't realize that my fellow graduate students can be so indoctrinated with exaggerations and propaganda blinding them to the reality of the situation. Let me explain several factors: availability of usable real estate, theory of slippery slope (if 5 miles from the WTC is too close then what happens if real estate is found 8 miles away? Where does it stop?), and condemning a religion because a radical sect carried out an atrocity.

Sophie: Shouldn't the Muslim congregation realize that they are connected in faith to the perpetrators? They should have realized that building a mosque there would inspire a reaction. I blame that religion for birthing and rearing those murderers. I distrust Muslim people.

Kim: I am confused by the connection that "middle eastern" means "terrorist" and that you have a hard time separating the ideas. I think you must understand that not all Middle Eastern people are terrorists, and that you can make an effort to stand up against such unfair assumptions.

Paul: I am somewhat surprised that one of my classmates is critical of the decision to build a religious and neighborhood center so close to the site of the towers. Did you know the congregation of the proposed mosque planned to spend the anniversary of September 11th in prayer for the lives lost and in hope for peace between Christians and Muslims?

Theresa: I don't care. I was living and working in downtown Manhattan on September 11, 2001. None of you will probably ever fear death from a terrorist—a terrorist who would be, most likely, Muslim.

Joanne: I am absolutely disgusted.... It makes me sad to be a Christian because I don't feel that way at all. In fact, I believe people should coexist. Gandhi said that he had no problem with Christ; rather, he had problems with Christians because they are so unlike Christ. It is moments like this that truly show what he was talking about. I don't believe Jesus would have done this for one second.... I know I like to think the best of humanity...but I have the hardest time being tolerant of intolerance.

Paul: I pray that vitriol-spewing "Christians" could get over their religious and ethnic biases to pray with the Muslims this year.

Sophie: I am so angry...and confused...and frustrated. We are told these "group process" sessions are a so-called chance to "dialogue" in a "non-judgmental" forum. I put those words in quotation marks because these are the words we used when we verbally promised to each other our agreement when we began the session. To which, I call bullshit!

Paul: I find it hard to repress my bile for those who hold personal opinions that do not accept and value all people.

Sophie: I have learned that we should not utter out loud our true, deep-in-the-gut feelings; and if we do, we're going to be judged for them. Those types of feelings are not acceptable in today's educated, enlightened, sensitive and aware university landscape.

Pretty Terrifying

Sophie, criticized and ostracized by her peers, was viewed as intolerant. Yet she was prepared to use these dialogue groups as an outlet for her "true, deep-in-the-gut feelings," for the intense emotions that can be stirred when conversing and learning about difference. Most students were "too polite" and did "not want to interrupt anyone," as Veronica wrote in her journal. One student noted that in most sessions "the same five people talked," and "many people did not feel comfortable sharing" (Leslie). This recognition is contrasted with admissions by several (as discussed above) that the "idea of feeling something other than my natural equilibrium is pretty terrifying" (Julia).

In the final group session, the facilitator asked group members to draw a picture that illustrated their feelings about the group process. Sophie reflected in her journal:

> I drew a picture of a table arrayed with chips and cookies (the facilitators fed us, for which I was always grateful). I was candid in my picture about what I got out of the group process. I felt none of us really shared anything of value. I felt we were too self-conscious of our words and how we would be perceived; we didn't want to stir the pot and upset anyone, so we all said the "correct" statements, answers and opinions.

She added that "Later, one of my classmates commended me for speaking the way I did, saying he too believed that no one, including himself, had really told the truth about how they felt about the sessions."

Despite the challenges and limitations, I still believe dialogue groups can become a "resonant box" wherein experiences and ideas meet the reactions of the listeners and together create a new story (Mirsky, 2008). The "resonant box," a term coined by Dinis, describes the empathic growth opportunity that a group setting can offer an individual (cited in Mirsky, 2008). While I have witnessed the reluctance and fear by my students to tell stories about themselves, I also observed their growing self-awareness through their reflective journaling, their readiness (by most) at the end of the semester to "become uncomfortable," to "not be afraid," and to "feel willing to act." The experience of being understood by others, as Julia felt when she realized some of her peers were also first-generation, low-income students, can open the way for personal growth.

Performing (Counter) Stories

I remain deeply committed to the potential of dialogue groups as a tool for students to listen and reflect on personal narratives. However, I also am aware that not all students feel free to verbalize their feelings and reactions, to tell improvisational stories. This illuminates the need for first-person narratives or other stories to be shared, even when students are reluctant. Performance and role playing offer a possibility. In addition to my use of film to spur dialogue, I will, in my future teaching, use reader's theatre, through which students can read from a "script" like the one above to illustrate misunderstandings and empathic failures and reveal defenses and resistances. These dramatic presentations can put a face on conflicts, personal biases, and assumptions. However, the use of stories alone is insufficient. As Kumagai and Lypson (2009), who argue the necessity to cultivate critical consciousness in the training of physicians, assert:

...to arouse empathy without simultaneously stimulating both critical reflection on one's own biases, privileges, and assumptions and acknowledgement of one's own personal responsibility to understand the causes of the suffering and seek effective solutions may lead a reader or listener to conclude, "yes, now I know what he/she/they experience" and leave it at that. (p. 785)

Thus, as students assume roles, either as readers or listeners, each projects his or her own subjective inner world through the experience—what Griffiths (2007) terms "being authentic"—increasing the possibility that the readers and listeners may be changed by the story; that through the performance of stories, one might re-examine one's place in the world. Their role playing allows them to perform a character who says things they feel nervous about saying, permits them to flout the rules and do the unexpected in a serious, academic space, and invites creative and playful transgressions of social norms (Griffiths, 2007).

A cautionary note: I am not suggesting some causal relationship whereby students, through use of dialogue groups and reflective writing, or even by incorporating performance and dramatic presentations, will demonstrate deeper and critical self-awareness or articulate empathic responses to others. Students must be willing to look at the self in those deep inner spaces that some people/students are unable to go. Without a developmental readiness to encounter the unfamiliar and to turn "a critical gaze on one's own values, assumptions, experiences, and opinions and questioning the moral validity of the state of affairs in the world" (Kumagai & Lypson, 2009, p. 786), no pedagogical techniques will yield (lasting) change. However, I suggest that the instructional strategies described here can invite people to be more curious and imaginative about the self, to consider our social performances, and to script and rehearse possibilities for other performances. As poet Grace Nichols (1984) writes:

I have crossed an ocean
I have lost my tongue
from the root of the old one
a new one has sprung.

Note
All names are pseudonyms, and students' consent was secured through human subjects approval process.

References

Gitlin, A. (2005). Inquiry, imagination, and the search for a deep politic. *Educational Researcher*, *34*(3), 15–24.

Griffiths, M. (2007). Keeping authenticity in play—Or being naughty to be good. In D. Orr, D. Taylor, E. Kahl, K. Earle, C. Rainwater, & L.L. McAlister (Eds.), *Feminist politics: Identity, difference, and agency* (pp. 119–140). Lanham, MD: Rowman & Littlefield.

James, J.H. (2008). Autobiography, teacher education, and (the possibility of) social justice. *The Journal of Curriculum & Pedagogy, 4*(2), 161–176.

Johnson, A. (2006). *Privilege, power and difference* (2nd ed.). New York: McGraw Hill.

Kumagai, A.K., & Lypson, M.L. (2009). Beyond cultural competence: Critical consciousness, social justice, and multicultural education. *Academic Medicine, 84*(6), 782–787.

Mirsky, J. (2008). The use of narrative analysis and psychoanalytic exploration of group process in multicultural training. *International Journal of Applied Psychoanalytic Studies, 5*(1), 2–15.

Nichols, G. (1984). *The fat black woman's poems.* London: Virago.

Nieto, S. (1999). *The light in their eyes: Creating multicultural learning communities.* New York: Teachers College Press.

Pope, R., Reynolds, A., & Mueller, J. (2004). *Multicultural competence in student affairs.* San Francisco, CA: Jossey-Bass.

Reid, F. (Producer/Director). (1995). *Skin deep* [documentary film]. San Francisco: California Newsreel.

Smith, L.M. (Producer). (2003). Episode 3: The house we live in. In L. Adelman (Executive Producer), *Race: The power of an illusion* [documentary film]. San Francisco: California Newsreel.

U.S. Commission on Civil Rights. (1981). The problem: Discrimination. Reprinted in P. Rothenberg (2001), *Race, class, and gender in the United States: An integrated study* (5th ed., pp. 255–265). New York: Worth Publishers.

Weems, M. (2003). *Public education and the imagination-intellect: I speak from the wound in my mouth.* New York: Peter Lang.

three

Anarchic Thinking in Acupuncture's Origins
The Body as a Site for Cultivating Imagination-Intellect

Mitra Emad

cupuncture's birthday in the United States was July 26, 1971, when The *New York Times*' foreign correspondent, James Reston, accompanied President Richard Nixon to China. During the visit Reston required an emergency appendectomy and received acupuncture needling for post-operative pain. He wrote about his experience in a front-page feature story in the *Times* that generated interest and excitement in the United States for alternatives to biomedical health care. The American media carried splashy stories about acupuncture, among other "exotic" health care alternatives throughout the early 1970s (cf. *Newsweek*, August 14, 1972) and the AMA-documented patient questions and demands for new types of care, including acupuncture (cf. American Medical Association Archives, Chicago, IL).

On the ground, in everyday practice, America's counter-culturalists were already busy bringing this new treatment modality into the context of social justice movements newly concerned with providing health care for all. A nurse in Chicago, volunteering at a free clinic during her off hours, a young couple immersed in California's back-to-the-land communal living, and an American student with a newly minted French philosophy doctorate, all found themselves compelled by and engaged with acupuncture during this hey-day of acupuncture's introduction into American health care. As an ethnographer observing their practice and hearing their stories, I find in them exemplars of Gail Stenstad's (1988) notion of "anarchic thinking," a practice of cultivating an "alertness for the presence of the strange within the familiar" (1988, p. 89), ultimately radically decentering the familiar. In their stories, it is the acupuncture needle and its propensity to "pin you down to be with yourself" (Karen Levine, interview, 1992) that opens up the possibility of the body's anarchic terrain. Beginning with the body is often the path towards what Homi Bhabha calls "newness entering the world" (1994, chapter 11). Mary Weems (2003) has developed a powerful notion of the imagination-intellect and its potential to revitalize and revolutionize public education. For purposes of this essay, I find it fascinating that Weems begins and ends her elucidation of the imagination-intellect with the human body:

> Like the human heart and its arteries, the imagination and intellect are inextricably linked; they develop simultaneously and, I suggest, one is not possible without the other.... I posit that...all ideas are first imagined, then intellectually developed in an interconnected process which mirrors the blood's circulation through the body, and like blood, this connection is essential to what Hofstader describes as the intellectual-life. (Weems, 2003, p. 1)

Weems's theory demands that we cultivate anarchic thinking for something new to enter the world. The creative and the rational, both at full strength, both set to a common pursuit, cooperating to achieve justice—this is exactly what I find in the following three stories of America's "original" acupuncturists.

I believe we can find in these stories a model for delineating and revitalizing the imagination-intellect in and through the body. In each of the stories, social justice through health care for all is enacted through bodily engagements with imagination-intellect and cultivates the wildness of anarchic thinking. However, none of the "characters" in the story are monolithic. What counts as "social justice," what sets anarchic thinking into motion, and the specific circulations of imagination-intellect differ tellingly in each story. In these specificities of difference, engaging the three stories that follow itself becomes a practice of imagination-intellect.

Story 1: A Nurse Discovers Acupuncture

Abbie Dring began working as an R.N. in 1967 and by the early 1970s chose to volunteer at one of Chicago's free clinics, a choice that she found "a lot more politicizing" than she expected.

> So I worked there starting about '71 or '70, and there was a group that ran it called Rising Up Angry. They were a grass-roots organization that was in Chicago that had a newspaper, and basically the premise was that health care was a human right and not a privilege—you know, only to the rich or those who can afford it. To that end, they had a lot of programs. One was people's law. There were a lot of different programs. And one was the clinic. In there I worked with probably about 15 other people who helped run the clinic. It was all volunteer.

And nobody got charged; no patient had to pay to go there. (Abbie Dring, interview, Chicago, May 31, 1991.)

In 1974, Rising Up Angry sponsored a street fair in Chicago's Lincoln Park district, and it was here that Abbie first encountered acupuncture. Both the treatment she received and the comments and explanations offered by the man in the booth galvanized her to engage with acupuncture herself.

> So what I did was I got a book and read about acupuncture. It was a real simple book. I believe it was Principles of Acupuncture and Moxibustion. And I carried it everywhere. And I remember going through it, and people would say, oh I have a headache, and I would say, press these points, press these points; oh I have cramps, oh I have this, oh I have that. And it worked. As I did it more and more and I could see how it helped people, I realized that I needed to learn this. (Abbie Dring, interview, 1991)

Without an official training institution—the Midwest College of Oriental Medicine was not founded until 1979—Abbie found a Korean practitioner through her street fair connection and began to study acupuncture with him 3 nights per week for 2 years. She found herself drawn particularly to how acupuncture "just made sense" rather than the ways in which it was "this different fun thing." Acupuncture's sense-making resonated with frustrations she experienced working as a nurse, especially at the free clinic, where she was "the highest person there." Doctors came and went, but Abbie and the other volunteers ran specimens to the lab, stayed to clean up the clinic, and often became the listeners for patients talking about their medical problems and wanting to know why they had ulcers, headaches, or whatever chronic problems they were presenting with at the clinic. Patients wanted to know what to do about their problems or what to take, and Abbie felt hampered by knowing which antibiotics or other pharmaceuticals would be helpful, but not being allowed to write prescriptions. She also felt that the explanatory models she was working with in Western medicine did not provide the type of answers people were looking for.

> And that was very frustrating. What I found in acupuncture was that it explained things in a way that people could understand. They'll say for example, they have headaches, and when they describe the type it is, I'll say that's damp congestion or that's your energy rising. And they'll say, yeah, yeah. Or you're stuck in the middle or something. People related to it; people understood it. I liked that. It made a lot of sense to me. It made me feel good. Plus I could do something about it. Even if it was only pressing on points. And that I liked too. I didn't like being under doctors, because being a nurse, I would see all the problems that doctors would create. It was very scary. The more I was in a hospital, the less I wanted to be in them. It was just the last place I'd want to be if I was sick. (Abbie Dring, interview, 1991)

Abbie's frustration with not being able to provide either satisfactory explanations or treatments for her patients at the free clinic allows her imagination-intellect to be awakened. Something new enters her world—the viability of acupuncture as a practice and an epistemology. Abbie's imagination-intellect develops outside the institution of a biomedical clinic, depending upon the cultivation of wildness, as delineated by Gail Stenstad:

> I want to…take seriously the suggestion that thinking which would be both subversive…and creative would be wild thinking: thinking which goes beyond conventional boundaries, deviates from expected goals and methods, and is not accounted for or predicted by any theory. This thinking will be, in a word, un-ruled or anarchic. (1988, p. 87)

For Abbie, being able to provide explanations that "people related to; people understood it" emerges from the creative force of engaging with acupuncture, which as a registered nurse is an activity that "deviates from expected goals and methods" (Stenstad, 1988) and lands Abbie in an un-ruled, anarchic world. Anarchy here is not an "anything goes" proposition. Rather, if we follow Stenstad's notion of anarchy as a philosophical practice, we can see that while Abbie's engagement with acupuncture is "rule-less," anarchic thinking is "nevertheless precise and careful" (Stenstad, 1988, p. 88). Stenstad's recombinant potion of creativity and subversion resonates with Weems's elixir of imagination and intellect. Both run "wild" with the predictability of how a health care practitioner (a nurse) is supposed to function within a health care institution (a biomedical clinic). And wildness feels good. It feels good because creativity and subversion flow together, because the heart pumping blood through the circulatory system and back into the heart mirrors the imagination pumping the intellect and the intellect coursing energy back to the imagination.

For Abbie, the wildness of choosing to operate outside the clinic, to offer hands-on treatment and explanations people could engage their own imagination-intellects around felt good: "I liked that. It made a lot of sense to me. It made me feel good. Plus I could do something about it." Abbie's sense of self-efficacy is awakened through the development of an imagination-intellect in the wilds of discovering acupuncture.

Story 2: Bringing Acupuncture to the Commune

The northern California wilderness offers a more literal notion of wildness as the biotic environment for cultivating imagination-intellect. In archival footage from the documentary film *Commune* (Berman, 2005), there is a scene from the early 1970s in which Harriet Beinfield and Efrem Korngold sit outside, naked, surrounded by acupuncture charts and a case of tiny needles, quietly discussing acupuncture points. This image encapsulates the flow of the imagination-intellect, as well as its ground in the body. In the early 1970s Harriet and Efrem found themselves living on one of California's first communes (and the only one that has lasted to the present), realizing that "one of the things we had to learn was how to do our own health care" (Efrem Korngold, interview, August 25, 2003). Both were already activists with strong ties to the feminist, civil rights, and anti-war social movements of the 1960s and 1970s. As the daughter and granddaughter of Jewish physicians, Harriet notes that a powerful ethos of social justice pervaded her childhood and young adulthood:

> I felt as if I grew up in an atmosphere of privilege, and that my father's implicit message to me was—I am affording you all the benefits that a young woman could have, and in return I don't want you to let something like the Holocaust happen to anyone anywhere. It's our duty to make the world a place fit for human habitation. (Harriet Beinfield, interview, August 25, 2003)

Imagining a just world and acting to carry it out brought both Harriet and Efrem to Black Bear (where they met), a commune established in the late 1960s around the motto "free land for free people." Building a socially experimental lifestyle, commune members as a whole were already learning from local miners, ranchers, loggers, and Native Americans about natural medicine, herbs, and wild foods.

> We were charged in this group that we lived with—there were sixty of us living together. We were charged with figuring out how to maintain our own survival. And, we were sort of cultural anthropologist adventurers who were looking at all the items of our culture that we felt were useful and the ones that we thought were not. (Harriet Beinfield, interview, 2003)

This counter-cultural sifting through contemporary and marginalized cultural practices as well as building alliances across social categories in search of useful skills and paradigms of a just society were core values at Black Bear that decentered the familiar and allowed newness to enter the world in the form of acupuncture. Firing up the imagination-intellect by paring daily life back to the most immediate survival skills quickly led the group to attend to health care. In the early 1970s, Efrem joined a group of community members who set out to learn more professional medical skills.

At that time, Efrem's father, Murry Korngold, was working in London as a pioneer in the field of clinical psychology and invited his son to visit and meet the acupuncturist who had helped him deal with his own severe depression. After meeting the founder of one of the major "schools" of acupuncture in the West, Jack Worsley, Efrem and Harriet gathered funds (including the results of Murry's successful round of card playing in Reno and a support loan from a Jewish foundation in San Francisco set up to help young people receive training in health care) and became students of the famed Worsley. While they've since separated their own version of acupuncture from Worsley's, they are both now credited as major influences in bringing the "five elements" style of acupuncture to the United States.

Unlike Abbie, Harriet and Efrem already have an awakened imagination-intellect, seeking to re-form a social world based on a holistic vision of what it means to be human. In their public life, the couple often act as a single persona (as they did in their interview with me), working, speaking, and writing in tandem as advocates for a holistic vision in which acupuncture can function as a network out of which the whole health of the social body can be addressed. Their persona functions optimally through an imagination-intellect embedded in activism.

> I think that certainly my interest and I think Harriet's interest in Chinese medicine emerged directly from our ideology that we were developing that was based on activism. You know, we actively engaged with the community that we were in to change, to reform that community and ourselves in the process to make it a place that is non-violent, that's enjoyable, that's pleasurable, that's, you know, nurturing to everything that makes human beings the wonderful creatures that we can be. And, it was clear that health care, medicine, as much as anything else, was a part of that. It was essential to make that happen. (Efrem Korngold, interview, 2003)

Imagination functions as the pumping heart of Harriet and Efrem's imagination-intellect. The project of envisioning a better world leads them to seek intellectual purchase in Chinese medicine to fuel the vision of a healthy, just society.

This movement from imagination to intellect and back again relies on acupuncture offering an embodied ground for activism. While Harriet and Efrem engage a vibrant imagination to envision their goals of social justice activism as an ideology of a perfect world, they actually build the social world in which human being is enjoyable and non-violent, and they do it just by thinking anarchically. Cultivating wildness through the recombinant flow of creativity and subversion, anarchic thinking for Harriet and Efrem emerges readily from the counter-cultural impetus of Black Bear ranch and the ethics of commune life.

> But what we were trying to make was not a profession. We came in it as counter-cultural, we like questioning medicine, we want to countervail against it, and all that it represented. Not because it was bad to have surgery when we had an accident, but because of the system. (Efrem Korngold, interview, 2003)

Efrem goes on to eloquently delineate that the "vision" of social justice—"*seeing* how things can be better" (emphasis added) grows from the well-tended, healthy body. Social justice and the power to change society require health care for all and are essentially bodily propositions for Efrem and Harriet:

> You know—where did the term empowerment come from? It came from us. We wanted to give power back to the people. And where does power come from? It comes from your own body. It comes from health, and from having your own will available to you, it comes from having your mind available to you, it comes from your ability to see clearly available to you. And knowing what the right thing to eat is; so all these fundamental things empower people: make you powerful, give you access to your own strength. And when you have that, then you want things to be different. That is the natural consequence of feeling good: then you see how things can be better. (Efrem Korngold, interview, 2003)

As in Stenstad's (1988) notion of anarchic thinking, Efrem and Harriet do not engage in subversion for the sake of subversion; wildness is not an "anything goes" party. The precision and care required by engaging with acupuncture to strengthen and empower human bodily being is wildly creative and requires both the imagination and the intellect for sustenance.

Story 3: Understanding Foucault from the Bronx

If imagination is the heart of Harriet Beinfield and Efrem Korngold's cultivation of wildness in their engagements with acupuncture, the heart of Mark Seem's version of the imagination-intellect is certainly the intellect. While working on his doctorate in French Studies in the early 1970s, Mark Seem befriended a visiting Michel Foucault at SUNY-Buffalo, where Rockefeller funding had brought in philosophical luminaries like Claude Lévi-Strauss, Jacques Lacan, and Jacques Derrida, along with Foucault. Moving in the direction of a career as a Foucault scholar, Seem spent the third year of his doctorate in Paris studying with Foucault, who agreed to serve on his thesis committee. All of this backfired, as Foucault's work and cultural identity at that time were considered threatening to mainstream academia.

> Studying with Foucault…was suspect from universities' points of view. So, I had a lot of trouble getting hired when I graduated and he was always writing these great letters for me, calling places directly and he finally called me and said, "I think you're making a mistake by pushing so heavily, that you studied with me. You should let [someone else] be the one writing the letters…. I can tell you when I make these calls, that it's me they don't want in their environment." (Mark Seem, interview, July 16, 2002)

Fewer academic jobs in general and the realization that he may not have made an astute career move by following his intellectual heart and studying Foucault's work led Mark to question: "Do I really want to do this? Do I want to put myself in a context where I'm fighting for having studied with whom I studied with, for what I want to teach? So I was having second thoughts" (Mark Seem, interview, 2002).

Entering a drug detoxification clinic in the Bronx to listen to a lecture on acupuncture in 1977 changed Mark's career path. The African American and Puerto Rican drug counselors who had trained in acupuncture in Montreal were delighted at Mark's willingness to translate French acupuncture texts for them. Social justice activism in the context of the detox clinic meant applying new learning in an immediate way every day. As he read and translated the French texts and got to know the acupuncturists, Mark became increasingly interested in acupuncture, began to volunteer at the detox clinic, eventually joining the Quebec Institute of Acupuncture and ultimately founding a school himself (first in Connecticut, then in New York City). This story, like the previous two, highlights the body as a site for cultivating imagination-intellect, but it also reveals a subtextual story in which the intellect functions as the heart pumping wildness to a subversive/creative imagination.Looking for any kind of intellectual work that could help him earn a living, Mark began to translate classical acupuncture texts for the Montreal acupuncture school. The school's founder, Oscar Wexu, asked him to translate the work of Nguyen Van Nghi, a Vietnamese medical doctor who had translated classical Vietnamese acupuncture texts into French. In exchange for a scholarship to the Quebec Institute of Acupuncture, Mark agreed to translate this major work. A prolific writer, on the forefront of brokering acupuncture into North American health care contexts, Mark has written about the intellectual transition from his Ph.D. work to acupuncture practice, again highlighting the intellectual pull of "meridian" acupuncture:

> This move from French philosophy to French acupuncture was an effortless one for me, as it took me right into the middle of medical anthropological matters akin to Foucault's work.... While the English-language translations of texts from the People's Republic of China (PRC) bored me with their obvious political indoctrination, the French texts carefully scrutinized the entire human energetic story of pathways that could be influenced by external stimulation. (Seem, 1992, p. 17)

Thinking anarchically, as Stenstad specifies, entails looking for the presence of the strange in the familiar, and Mark's training in French philosophical critiques of contemporary culture, particularly medical culture, influenced his reading of the classical acupuncture texts he was engaged in translating into English. The French texts, often originating in Vietnam rather than China, emphasized what Mark later came to call "acupuncture energetics" (Seem, 1987)—the movement of qi (loosely translatable as "energy") along meridians traversing the body. Mark likened his reading of these classical acupuncture texts with studying Foucault's delineation of The Birth of the Clinic (1973/1963) as an epistemic rupture from traditional, pre-modern, humoral medicine.

Mark's intellectual fascination with acupuncture's philosophical map of the body yields its own epistemic rupture as he moves back and forth between reading/translating and beginning to learn acupuncture's clinical practice:

> Well, it fascinated me immediately, just immediately.... What attracted me was just seeing it, because I went up [to the clinic in the Bronx] and they started teaching. I was fascinated. In fact when they started teaching, I opened Foucault's Birth of the Clinic because he had some wild sections that I had a hard time following where he talked about [how] the atlas for the human body has not always been constructed the same way as ours. [Foucault describes how] modern analysis is constructed with the dotted lines that the surgeon's going to take, because we know he knows what he's going to find in there now, so this dotted line anatomy that makes modern Western clinical science possible, is not the anatomy that was happening before that became the way we know about the body. [The Birth of the Clinic] gives us some quotes from 17th- or 18th-century medicine, talking about vapors and fluids: the vapors drying up, the fluids drying up and the vapors getting trapped and this happening that happening in the patient. The description of things happening in the patient; it sounded preposterous! And, I'd read it with fascination, but I couldn't quite relate to it; I wasn't trained in medicine at all, didn't have any medical background. Then all of a sudden, here I was in the Bronx watching these Black and Puerto-Rican acupuncturists doing this Chinese practice, treating poor patients who had never heard of acupuncture. (Mark Seem, interview, 2002)

The movement from intellect to imagination in Mark's simple statement about going to the Bronx clinic to learn acupuncture and immediately opening a book—"In fact when they started teaching, I opened Foucault's Birth of the Clinic..."—demonstrates the intellect as the beating heart of Mark's engagement with acupuncture. Ultimately his imagination is fired by the intellectual work of radicalizing the strange within the familiar as it shows itself in clinical practice:

> [Many of these patients] didn't like needles and many of them were addicts or families of addicts so here's needles being used on people who use needles. This is the weirdest cultural thing I've ever seen in my life. It was. And, they'd stick the needles in and the patient would start saying, "Whoa, oh boy! That's it!" And, I was amazed because I was very much an anthropologist kind of person and in the book, it says you are supposed to needle until there is deh Qi which means qi is moving. But, the teachers didn't tell you that qi was moving yet. So, I was just trying to figure out if this was real or if it was a metaphor. What is all this stuff I was studying? (Mark Seem, interview, 2002)

This section of the interview beautifully evokes an imagination-intellect embodied and full of life: moving from "the book" to his teachers needling patients to the patients exclaiming "that's it!" the elements of imagination and of intellect are both at full strength, yielding an anarchic wildness rooted in bodily being:

> Black and Puerto Rican patients are not near as reserved as white middle-class patients, who were the ones that I was more used to and they would just say what they were feeling. And they would say, "I am feeling that move up here and this is happening, I am getting a little bit light headed, but I am also getting this and I am feeling my gut start to go and in fact it is just gurgling," and they'd just go on and on and on about, "Oh and that one did that and that one did this." Puerto Rican patients would often see visions. They would have these spirits come in the room, and they would say, "Oh this is coming in and that's okay, that's a healing vision." So I just thought that it was the wildest thing I had ever seen in my life, and I started getting what Foucault was talking about. (Mark Seem, interview, 2002)

As the familiar ground of the body rapidly becomes decentered for Mark, the flow from intellect to imagination and back again moves away from "the book" and rests ultimately in the realm of the body and of patients' bodily experiences:

> Here was a system of medicine talking about the body and carving it up totally differently. These people weren't being taught it. So it's not like they needed to know the language or the metaphor because no one was saying to them its yin and yang and the five phases or even meridians or anything. And they were having a transformative experience. Their bodies were not afraid to go along with what was happening. And, they expressed amazement. But, they also very frequently immediately believed in this medicine. It was like "something's happening, [so] I believe it." (Mark Seem, interview, 2002)

Conclusions: Setting Anarchic Thinking into Motion

Like many acupuncture patients in North America (cf. Emad & Cassidy, 2001, and Emad, forthcoming), the patients Mark Seem observed at the detox clinic found that feeling is believing. The sensation that "something is happening" led not only to expressions of amazement, but also to "very frequently immediately believ[ing] in this medicine." For Mark, watching this process, observing the patients feel reinvigorated when they were lethargic and calmed when they were wired, seeing is believing. In both cases (the patient and the fledgling practitioner) the body has set anarchic thinking into motion—for the patients, the strange sensations in the familiar body; for the practitioner, the metaphor that is not one, but rather a bodily knowing—both are "alert for the presence of the strange within the familiar" (Stenstad, 1988, p. 89).

Gail Stenstad asks: "What sets anarchic thinking into motion?" and in her philosophical response lies a resonance with the three stories of an awakened imagination-intellect: "Anything which deeply concerns us, touches us in mind and heart, provokes thinking…. It could be some oppressive situation calling for action, or the success of an act of resistance to oppression. It might be the touch of a hand or the sound of a voice" (Stenstad, 1988, p. 88). While the shape of justice is not the same in all three stories told in this essay, the notion that justice must be grown and nurtured from a healthy body "deeply concerns" each practitioner, touching her or him "in mind and heart, provok[ing] thinking" (Stenstad, 1988, p. 88). The call to act in the face of this concern brings anarchic thinking to fruition and engages imagination-intellect in the project of freeing human being.

References

Berman, J. (Director). (2005). *Commune* [documentary film]. Encinitas, CA: Five Points Media.

Bhabha, H. (1994*). The location of culture*. New York: Routledge.

Emad, M. (forthcoming). *Twirling the needle: The body as a site for cultural translation in American encounters with acupuncture*. Albany: State University of New York Press.

Emad, M., & Cassidy, C. (2001). What patients say about Chinese medicine. In C. Cassidy (Ed.), *Contemporary Chinese medicine and acupuncture*. New York: Churchill-Livingstone.

Foucault, M. (1973). *The birth of the clinic: An archaeology of medical perception* (A. Sheridan, Trans.). New York: Pantheon. (Original work published 1963)

Newsweek. (1972, August 14). All about acupuncture [cover feature story].

Seem, M. (1987). *Acupuncture energetics*. Rochester, VT: Healing Arts Press.

Seem, M. (1992). American acupuncture comes of age: Perspectives from the frontlines. *Medical Acupuncture Journal*, 4(2), 16–23.

Stenstad, G. (1988). Anarchic thinking. *Hypatia*, 3(2), 87–100.

Weems, M. (2003). *Public education and the imagination-intellect: I speak from the wound in my mouth*. New York: Peter Lang.

Interviews

All interviews were conducted by the author.

Beinfield, Harriet. Butler Creek Community, Somes Bar, California, August 25, 2003.

Dring, Abbie. Private acupuncture practice, Chicago, Illinois, May 31, 1991.

Korngold, Efrem. Butler Creek Community, Somes Bar, California, August 25, 2003.

Levine, Karen. AnHao Natural Health Care Center, Portland, Oregon, August 1992.

Seem, Mark. Tri-State College of Acupuncture, New York City, July 16, 2002.

ꞏᶠour ꞏ

Call and Response
Writing to Answer the Urge of a Bruised Spirit

Dominique C. Hill

They called me.
Called for me. Told me,
I had work to do.
Be. Catalyst, they said.
Said id spilled my blood too many times
Let men hurt me   too   many times
Been walked over   too   many times
Cried   too   many times
Hurt myself   too   many times
Damn
Love
I let her
him
my fifth grade teacher
them
convince me
urge me
        Bleed
        THIS   TIME—   I was to bleed life.
They came to me.
Summoned me. Tasked me,

to break again, to be healed.
To begin again.
Came in my sleep, and when I awoke,
tears covered my face,
confirming my purpose.
Rebel!
Be!
Dance!
Write!, they said.
Declared comfort a luxury
Said

    Deep   inside
          Wounds   Opened
    THIS   TIME—   in search of healing

They called me, I answered.
Memories, struggles,
to be—black, she, poet, aggressive me, flooded,
my body
I cried.
Yelled.
Stood frozen.
Began to write.
A story, my story, of a/my healing journey.

* * *

Imbued in the above prose is the assertion that my scholarship is more than research, publications, and highbrow conversation to be read only by those in academia. More than an arrogant pursuit to "give voice" by telling my interpretations of the experiences of others. And more than an attempt to validate or be validated. This is a journey of healing—of self, and subsequently communities to which I belong and do not belong, academe, and society. A firm believer that the self is integral to understanding and transformation, and that the self initiates or stifles healing, this piece is an embodied story of the relationship between my body and schooling. Simultaneously, this embodied text extends my individual black female body into the collective, situating this text as a telling of struggles, resistance, wounds, and healing embodied by both myself and the black female collective.[1]

As such, when referring to speaking flesh, this flesh symbolizes physical and discursive elements of black femaleness. Here, such speech emerges from my experience, located within an ongoing and living history of female of color adversity, rebellion, and telling placing our individual stories into a collective reality. Drawing on the genius of feminist-of-color writings in *This Bridge Called My Back*[2] (Moraga & Anzaldua, 1983), flesh is a cellar storing and holding memories, histories, wounds, and inconvenient truths. Also, flesh is the knowledge, stories, and pains from which I/we speak. So when the flesh speaks, the house, e.g., school, institutions, the self, status quo, is destabilized, igniting an interruption—a moment of potential transformation.

Recognizing that transformation requires a 'naming' of injustice, I offer a metaphor of the union that is embedded in the fabric of our society and thus schooling. Then, present poetry in motion,[3] reflective of and yet resistant to the union. Next, in a letter to my fifth-grade teacher, I "talk back"[4] to schooling. Lastly, I distinguish between schooling and skoolin' and offer directions for continuing the journey toward healing.

'Til Death Do Us Part: An Unholy Union— Racism, Sexism, Heteropatriarchy, and Schools[5]

Heteropatriarchy: Racism, do you take sexism to be your lawfully wedded partner in crime? To promise to love, cherish, and honor sexism? To live by the word of Hetero and support sexism in all endeavors that reflect the law of the land? To respect her wishes when they align with your own and result in the production of over-categorization of bodies, narrowly defined conceptions of maleness and femaleness, preserve whiteness as property, and demand compartmentalization of identities?

Racism: I do.

Heteropatriarchy: To have, to hold, to tame, to direct, to complete, to distort, and minimally respect? 'Til death do you part?

Racism: I do.

Heteropatriarchy: And sexism, do you take racism to be your lawfully wedded partner in crime? To promise to love, cherish, and honor racism? To live by the word of Hetero and support racism in all endeavors that reflect the law of the land? To honor and obey? To align your hopes and dreams with racism when they maintain the power of Hetero and result in mental and physical imprisonment, synthetic progress, communal chaos, token slots of power, and early mortality?

Sexism: I do

Heteropatriarchy: To have, to hold, to complete, to submit to, to distort, and respect? 'Til death do you part?

Sexism: I do.

Heteropatriarchy: Then by the power in Me and this great society, I now pronounce you eternal partners in crime. You may now birth communities that battle one another, exclusionary organizations invested in "either/or" mentalities, societal leaders who rank oppressions, institutions that carry your blood in their walls, and schools that devalue females and bodies of color.

Despite attempts by informal policies and social realities to present these ideologies as separate and in competition, I knew they could not, should not be compartmentalized or ranked. Moreover, I knew they informed each other and demanded the others' existence. What I was less sure of were their implications for my future work in education. Around the same time I wrote the union piece, my adviser posed the question: "Where do you stand?" Confident in the union's destruction, aware of the harm it caused but less affirmed in the *now what?* I froze. Over time and through tears, conversations invoking painful memories, and writing, I thawed and took a stance—my flesh spoke:

> I am not invested in factorymanufacturedbodies and identities. Not interested in a one-size-fits-all approach to education. Nor am I committed to a fragmented look at bodies and people. Change requires more than thinking about it. And I do not intend to simply sit and think. I presume the body is comprised of mind-physicality-the knowledge created withinandfrom it. Yet, the popular belief is the body and mind are separate. Assuming the body a devalued and often unintelligible place, I am more interested in the potential nuance of seeing the body and situating the body as more than. More thananirrationalbundleofnerves and fleshandbone. More than a thing to be gawkedatnjudged. More than thatwhich has been given credit to the body. MybodyAblackfemalebodythisblackfemalebody.

A Reflection:
I Remember When I Moved to the Sound of the Djembe

S   l   o   w
                            ly
and
SURELY
I am coming   Remembering that I
              into

          myself.,   perhaps in my former life—
                                      infancy—maybe
                                      everywhere but here,
                          moved first.

Danced
Walked
Ran
Jumped
Expressed   and then,
                   if at all,

                          THOUGHT
      'Bout what it all meant. I had to, cuz I'm a thinker.
Somewhere
M y m o v e ment   had meaning
                              had value—
                                    had   ME in it.
                                                       Now
sitting in these
academia
walls of
                              between
reading and teaching
                                    trying to be and justifying how I be
      I have to concentrate on M.O.V.E.ment.
      Though I confess a lil' less than those first fours year
      less than in high school.
      What's important is I receive zero
      pay for doing the work of teachers
                          schools   society.
                          Family
I participant-observeself-scrutinizejudgemonitor
                   since I don't know when.
What   I   DO   know
      This regulating and evaluating
      has gone onnnnnnnnnnnnnnnnn
      Still exist.   Maybe forever
      I am adding unlearning
            Relearning
            Deconstructing and reimagining
      to this unpaid position—claiming it as a career.
      The ugliness and harm done to the self   at the hand of

ideologies—structures—teachers' "best practices" and—
Internalization of it all.
With all this
                    W   E   I   G   H   T
On   my back
Imprinted on
            myblackcollegeeducatedfemale working-class with middle class
capitalqueertrying-to-make-ends-meet
                    body
    I   Tell
                Remember
                Write
                Choreograph
                                        Me, her, and her, and their
    relationship to the environment around us.

                            * * *

The preceding performative text embodies emotions, process, and the journey I
am on to explicate my body as (my)self. Through movement on the page, broken
words, and fluidity in possible text reading directions, I offer my visual through
schooling and healing. Important to this piece are the tensions and potential rec-
onciliation evidenced. Equally pertinent is the realization through this piece that
a deeper understanding of the impact of schooling on the *body* [6] may be attained
with reflections around schooling processes, unspoken normatives in schooling,
and responses to identity performances. Present in the text above is the assertion
that processes of schooling draw mythical lines and divisions between mind and
body. Furthermore, this false mind-body split results in mechanical, perhaps in-
authentic movement intended to signify accomplishment.

Yet academic accomplishment is not determined by behavior. Nor is academic success a direct outcome of what is deemed good behavior. Instead, behavior considered acceptable speaks more to the ability of a person, in this case a
student, to follow standard rules and codes—some verbalized, some not—around
proper student conduct. However, more times than not black students generally,
and black female students particularly, are evaluated on our behavior usually read
as indicative of academic ability or failure. [7] Painfully aware of this assessment on
both a personal and collective level of black females, I felt compelled to write.
Those before me urged me to speak and exclaimed that my silence would not save
me or any one else.[8] My spirit cried for the djembe. Moved by the quaking in my
cellar, I started to write.

Aint Nothin' Righteous about Schooling When They in Charge:
A Letter to My Fifth-Grade Teacher

January 2011

Greetings Mr. Dodd.

I hope this finds you well. I am sure you are surprised to hear from me, but this letter is necessary—for your ears, for my spirit, and for the future of education.[9] I write this letter while sitting in the house of frustration, with walls of anger, on a foundation called determination, in search of newness. You may not remember me, the little black girl in your fifth-grade class—always asking questions, feeding Canterbury, one of our class rabbits, and Annie, the class tarantula. Do you recall telling me, "Shut up," and directing me physically with your hands to properly sit in a seat? Perhaps you remember using the word stupid to describe some of my friends? No? But I remember. I remember your pale face turning the color of your red off-kilter toupee, your impatience, and your body language that indicated indifference at best and disgust at worst. In case you were wondering, the notion that I/we your students would not get far in life still dwells with me. Sometimes it manifests in self-doubt, fatigue, tears, and other times rage, ideas, and innovation.

To be clear, the intent of this letter is not to fill you with guilt until you implode or remind you of how you belittled and mentally assaulted many black children's colorful spirits. Nor is this simply about my ability to surmount the bullshit I internalized and carry with me daily on the likes of your teaching. These realities influenced my interest in writing this letter, but I am more interested in expressing my awareness, once naivete, that there are *so many* of you in the world. I also write to thank you for igniting in me a fire to be critical of the "education" I receive and hopefully eliminate the miseducation and damaging of souls and spirits prompted by Mr. Dodd. I am writing for justice.[10] Surely, with your intellect you know that Mr. Dodds come in many packages—Mrs., Ms., white, Mexican, black, teachers, professors, bus drivers, and so on. *You are everywhere.* Watching me and scrutinizing my being.[11] Strongly suggesting or outright correcting how I/we move, what I/we say, don't say and how I/we say, and what I tell my students. Yes, I opted to be an educator and not a teacher, because unlike you I am more invested in transformation than imitation.

You see, Mr. Dodd, I realize that within a year under your tutelage, you sold me/us more than enough lies for me/us to drop out of school and succumb to a life of public assistance. You also painted a grim picture of our likely futures. The Mr. Dodds after you continued where you left off, trying to replace my aggressive nature with coyness and respectability. All of you tried to convince me the unholy union was nonexistent. That the tensions I felt and still feel dwelled only in my mind, declaring a war within myself between being black and female. Time and time again, Mr. Dodd, you all had me thinking I had to decide to be one or the other, when in reality I was both all along. You had me bowing to patriarchy simultaneously, though unaware, colluding with heteronormativity. Over and over I betrayed myself, my being, to fit into some neat idea passed down to you from the union. To top it off, even with self-betrayal, confusion, and damage to my spirit, you declared me mediocre at best and a future welfare or prison case more than likely.

Upon leaving your class, I was shattered. Schooling succeeded in demarcating a minimal place for me and ensured my ability to recognize it. "Education" failed me, but I did not lose hope altogether. I realized my spirit needed saving and the Mr. Dodds of this world and this schooling I received, could not aid in that process. Nor will I/we be saved by institutions that compartmentalize or malicious ideologies intended to destroy and pit people against each other and themselves. You know Mr. Dodd, aint no *just* savin' when they in charge. Nope! Cuz, aint-nothin' righteous about schooling when the union in charge. Aintnothin' fair, just, or equitable about anything that the unholy union runs. Can you smell that Mr. Dodd? There is a stench in the air. Whether intentional or happenstance, that funk of injustice speaks for itself. Do you smell that funk in the air, on your hands?!

At this juncture, you should feel: pain, guilt, remorse...*Something*! If you feel nothing, I pity you. Yet, pity is not going to restore the broken pieces of us who have suffered through schooling. Like air, it is omnipresent, and schooling's impact becomes apparent only in its temporary absence. With a taste of its absence, I learned of new possibilities. In those moments I also became enraged and painfully aware of the work you and other Mr. Dodds do. Even more so saddened that some Mr. Dodds are black women, peers, teachers and family members that I love and greatly respect. Even more gut wrenching, the realization that since Mr. Dodds are everywhere, you also resided within. The thought of you living in me makes me itch and in that initial moment made me want to rip myself open and tear out every itty-bitty piece of you—*if only* it were that simple.

I am no longer naïve to the world or the overt and internal workings of ideologies, standards of control, and (self) surveillance that encourage me/us to commit to the status quo of the day. More importantly, I recognize that I was schooled to work against myself and almost persuaded to spend my life trying to disown and desensitize myself to the djembe—to forbid my flesh from speaking. I also know that some Mr. Dodds are well meaning and this wounding I speak of was not always intentional. To reiterate, *impact* is the focus here. Mr. Dodd, you all will be held accountable for your doings. I respect that this letter may or may not have an impact on your sub-par behavior and thoughts. Furthermore, you may see little or nothing wrong with mentally assaulting students' self-concepts.

For all I know, your intention was to break down the spirits of black students, but only you know that answer. So this letter is *not* a request for your hand in saving me/us.[12] I am fully capable of and required to save myself/us to ensure our healing. Although I am not soliciting aid from you, you are not excused from your poor decisions or strategy, whichever description fits best. Nor are you all absolved from the outcomes of your actions directed by your allegiance to the union. This letter is to serve you formal notice that I am breathing new air, aware, active, and no longer afraid to allow my flesh to speak.

Regards,
Your former student

* * *

Reiterated through the above letter is the self as fundamental to healing and resistance. The letter to Mr. Dodd/s is a flesh-speaking moment in which I verbalize my brokenness and, in so doing, stimulate healing. As a former fifth-grade student in Mr. Dodd's class, the preceding letter serves as a skoolin' moment where I speak from my flesh, recounting the hurt and the journey through schooling. While specifically addressing the harm done in my fifth-grade class, I also mention the work of schooling throughout my life and the schoolers involved. Identifying those who enact schooling as family members, non-schoolteachers, women of color, and men situates schooling as something that takes place in as well as outside of schools.[13]

In contrast, skoolin' constitutes resistance to these processes as well as their outcomes that include but are not limited to: constrained performances of identity, reproduction of social hierarchies, bruised black female spirits, and false conflation of race and academic ability, to name a few. Skoolin' is committed to tellin' it like it is and acknowledging the ongoing work of healing. Together these qualities create a doorway into understanding bodies' relationship to schooling. Still, the question of *so what does this mean* may linger in the minds of some, and if skeptical or complicit enough, possibly pass through their lips.

School Me, No Skool You!: Continuing the Journey to Heal My Bruised Spirit

I have been and continue to be schooled at the hands of people invested, consciously or unconsciously, in the status quo. These same people are catalysts for self- and social critique. I resent and appreciate them. There is no simple way to explain the nature of my body's relationship to schooling. Nor are there hard, fixed descriptions to capture how black females experience schooling in our bodies. I gather that regardless of the specifics of our individual experiences, the aesthetics of these experiences are painted with constraint; narrow constructions of femininity; self-doubt; the fusion of behavior with academic success.[14] Even as I write, the embarrassment and disappointment of succumbing to such a process nearly paralyzed my journey, but my predecessors pleaded, "*Let your flesh speak.*" Acknowledging the ache of remembering the stories behind my wounds and then sharing them compels me to believe that an investment in healing bruised spirits at the hands of schooling begins with recognition of wounds.

I am wounded.
Five   years   ago I was uber black.
Four   years   ago I was an uber feminist.
                                                                 Three years ago I was hella-
                                                                         broken-hearted.
Two years ago, I was hella happy with myself
thought I had "found" myself.
                                                          One year ago, I was in love.
                                          Today
I am searching   Found,
Longing   to restore
                        some pieces of me I threw out along the way.
Didn't know I needed em.
Thought they were irrelevant.
                                          Now
                                                   I see
they are necessary
pieces of my life
my self, my journey
                 remind me of the path I walked.
                                          I am not what others want me to be
Not even what I want me to be   a combination of the two.
Cuz in the world I liv everything   s
                                          Connected
                                          close,

D   I   st
ant   familiar
strange

The above prose names some of the outcomes and forced choices to accommodate, impress, and please those schooling me. These decisions echo a need to conform and fit. Concomitantly, when hearing the djembe and waking in tears after a heart-to-heart with those who came before me while sleeping, Rebel! was their instructions.

> They called me, I answered
> with my whole heart.
> They called with the drums,
> and my body answered.
> I cried.
> Yelled.
> Stood frozen.
> Began to write,
> admit!, do!, be!,
> what they whispered to me.

"Wounded? *Let your flesh speak.*"

Notes

1. Referring to place of location and its connection to power regarding blackness and femininity. McKittrick (2006) suggests, "stories of black women contain in them meaningful geographic tenets, but these are often reduced to the seeable flesh and unseeable geographic knowledges" (p. 45). Recognition of such undermining that has and continues to occur is essential to understanding the importance of speech, writing as resistance, and the many ways being a black female necessitates daily boundary-crossing and spatial disruptions.

2. In the edited volume *This Bridge Called My Back: Writing of Radical Women of Color*, flesh is situated as generative of meaning. Moraga & Anzaldua (1983) assert, "A theory in the flesh means one where the physical realities of our lives—our skin color, the land or concrete we grew up on, our sexual longings—all fuse to create a politic born out of necessity. Here, we attempt to bridge the contradictions in our experience" (p. 23). These women purport experience of the flesh as primary knowledge rather than rules and normatives in the social sphere.

3. See Shange (1975).

4. See hooks (1994).

5. Drawing upon current state-sanctioned conceptions and popular understandings of marriage with which I grew up, the above dialogue describes an unholy union that I purport is mapped onto bodies and schooling processes. Interwoven throughout the unholy union described and their ideologies individually is control—the door through which schools enter. Since their construction, schools have served as gatekeepers, devising an illusory but felt line between the educated and uneducated, civilized and uncivilized, males and females, white and non-white, privileged and disenfranchised.

6. Appraisal of students' worth centers around the degree to which their identities and knowledge fit—or are assumed to fit—with the reigning standards and normatives. Students' bodies are put against the standards and become sites of evaluation. When considering the body and the production of the body, it is imperative to acknowledge that power, hierarchies, identities, values, ideologies, and structures permeate environments. Moreover, that human knowing as well as others' assumed knowledge of us get mapped, re-mapped, and implanted into our bodies—affecting self-concepts, knowledge, and the movement of its physicality (see Duncan, 1996; hooks, 1996; McKittrick, 2006; Pillow, 2004).

7. *Some supportive studies:*

Signithia Fordham's (1993) study set at a magnet program within a larger public school in Washington, DC, examines expectations surrounding feminine expression. Fordham found that the differential assessment of black girls' academic futures related to their gender performance and girls who faired best in school—good grades, test scores, and support from teachers—often took a more silent approach to their education. These "good" girls did not *disrupt* the assumed social order between black boys and girls. In contrast, those "loud black girls" tended to have good grades but lower test scores. This ethnographic study revealed that assumed gender roles and conceptions of femininity influenced the perception of black girls and demonstrated the strain black females feel while striving for academic success. Those girls who resisted behaviors deemed acceptable by teachers and other staff were marked assertive, budding black feminists—code for inferior, as indicated in the phrase "those loud black girls."

Linda Grant's (1994) study "Helpers, Enforcers, and Go-Betweens" examined six first-grade classrooms and the roles assigned to black girls in those settings. Grant argued that informal processes in the classroom introduce and/or encourage black girls to assume specific roles of "helper, enforcer, or go-between." She suggests that these roles assisted in shaping and preparing black girls for service-related work. Black girls' sociability was accepted and marked as a sign of their success in the future. When black girls performed average or below average in the class, their academic performance was attributed to their ability.

Edward Morris's (2007) 2-year ethnographic study explores the classroom experiences of black girls, and Morris concludes that the girls received punishment and/or suffered public shame for their "loud" and "un-lady like" behavior. To combat unfeminine conduct, the school developed an organization, The Proper Ladies, in which girls learned table etiquette, manners, and "how to be a lady." Morris noted the insistence by mostly female teachers of color that black girls be "ladies" and not "loudies." Morris observes that girls exhibiting self-reliance, outspokenness, and self-protection outnumbered and outscored all other students at the school on pre-advancement courses. In addition, these girls were more vocal than any other group of girls in math and science classes. Despite their average and sometimes above-average academic performance, black girls' "loudness" was a sign to teachers of tentative academic success.

8. See Lorde (1983).

9. In *Public Education and the Imagination-Intellect*, Mary Weems (2003) articulates through poetry and performance texts the connection between the personal, education, social change, and taking a stance. She states: "Education is essential to developing an activist, political stance" (p. xx). Placing her position into conversation with the intent of scholarship, my letter to Mr. Dodd, the collective, is a telling, an intentional disposition against my former schooling. This letter thereby serves as a skoolin' moment verbalizing the wounds produced by successful attempts by schooling practices to rip me of imagination.

10. In *All About Love: New Visions*, bell hooks (2000) states, "The heart of justice is truth telling, seeing ourselves and the world the way it is rather than the way we want it to be" (p. 33). As such, this letter writing re-memory of schooling experiences opens wounds associated with schooling. Concurrently, this opening—truth-telling creates the possibility of justice.

11. See Jill Scott, "Watching Me" (2001).

12. Resisting the tendency for research and programs for underrepresented students and girls to adopt a model of saving those individuals from ourselves and our inevitable destruction, I operationalize the practice of many black feminists and feminists of color that we must save ourselves. As a black female following the assertions by hip-hop feminist Ruth Nicole Brown (2009) that we, black girls old and young, are the experts of our experience, saving becomes a collective process by which we engage our social realities to heal and re-imagine ourselves emerging as who we want to be and not who others want us to be.

13. Schooling (Shujaa, 1998), works to sustain hierarchical relationships. Alongside maintenance of the status quo, schooling also presents a fictive erasure of the body and sustains narrow constructions of student success. While educational literature often situates education and schooling as synonymous processes, they are distinct concepts and seeing them as such helps to better explicate how black females uniquely experience and are sculpted by schooling. An example of

this maintenance of status quo is exhibited in the safeguarding of hierarchical relationships in the war generated between different groups of students (see AAUW, 2001, 2008).

Despite AAUW's commitment beginning in 1992 to addressing and unveiling gender disparities and differential experiences based on gender, it was not until their 2008 report, *Where the Girls Are: The Facts About Gender Equity in Education*, that achievement data was disaggregated by race and gender combined. This report discusses girls' educational achievement over the past 35 years. Data offered in *Where the Girls Are* come from the National Assessment of Educational Process (NAEP). Tests results, using a singular variable, through NCES, show that girls continue to outperform boys in reading, and boys outperform girls in math. Math and reading tests show a wider disparity in test scores by race than gender, with white students performing at the highest rates and African Americans the poorest—suggesting a major gap between boys and girls respectively.

Yet when disaggregating data from NAEP on race and gender, tests show white girls' test scores closest to white boys' than any other girls, black or Latina. Similarly, black girls' scores were closest to black boys', with black girls scoring only slightly lower than black boys on the standardized math test. Contrary to the rhetoric of "gender wars," the biggest gap between boys' and girls' test scores resided between white boys and white girls. Still, students' test scores proved closer within racial groups. These data indicate that the combination of race and gender creates a different story on the achievement of students than gender alone. The lack of interest in disaggregating data along race and gender lines implies a commitment to assessing the achievement of all children, with "all" referring to white students. Equally, this statistical analysis indicates a lack of space and value afforded to black girls specifically, and race-gendered analysis generally, along with a fictive erasure of the body in the schooling process.

14. See "Utopia" in Weems (2003); also Evans-Winters, 2005; Fordham, 1993; Henry, 1998; Horvat & Antonio, 1999; Lei, 2003; Morris, 2007.

References

American Association of University Women Educational Fund (1992). *How schools shortchange girls: The AAUW report.* Washington, DC: Author.

American Association of University Women Educational Fund (1998). *Gender gaps: Where schools still fail our children.* Washington, DC: Author.

American Association of University Women Educational Fund (2001). *Beyond "gender wars": A conversation about girls, boys, and education.* Washington, DC: Author. Retrieved from http://aauw.org/research/upload/BeyondGenderWar.pdf

American Association of University Women Educational Fund (2008). *Where the girls are: The facts about gender equity in education.* Washington, DC: Author. Retrieved from http://www.aauw.org/research/upload/whereGirlsAre.pdf

Brown, R.N. (2009). *Black girlhood celebration: Toward a hip-hop feminist pedagogy.* New York: Peter Lang.

Duncan, N. (1996). Renegotiating gender and sexuality in public and private space. In N. Duncan (Ed.), *BodySpace: Destabilizing geographies of gender and sexuality.* New York: Routledge.

Evans-Winters, V. (2005). *Teaching black girls: Resiliency in urban classrooms.* New York: Peter Lang.

Fordham, S. (1993). "Those loud black girls": (Black) women silence, and gender "passing" in the academy. *Anthropology and Education Quarterly, 32,* 3–32.

Freire, P. (1968). *Pedagogy of the oppressed.* New York: Continuum.

Grant, L. (1994). Helpers, enforcers, and go-betweens: Black females in elementary school classrooms. In M.B. Zinn & B.T. Dill (Eds.), *Women of color in U.S. society.* Philadelphia: Temple University Press.

Henry, A. (1998). "Invisible" and "womanish": Black girls negotiating their lives in an African-centered school in the USA. *Race Ethnicity and Education, 1*(2), 151–170.

hooks, b. (1990). *Yearning: Race, gender, and cultural politics.* Boston, MA: South End Press.

hooks, b. (1994). *Teaching to transgress: Education as the practice of freedom.* New York: Routledge.

hooks, b. (1996). *Bone black: Memories of girlhood.* New York: Henry Holt.

hooks, b. (2000). *All about love: New visions.* New York: Harper Perennial.

Horvat, E.M., & Antonio, A.L. (1999). "Hey, those shoes are out of uniform": African American girls in an elite high school and the importance of habitus. *Anthropology & Education Quarterly, 30*(3), 317–342.

Johnson, M. (2007). *The meaning of the body: Aesthetics of human understanding.* Chicago, IL: University of Chicago Press.

Lei, J.L. (2003). (Un)necessary toughness?: Those "loud black girls" and those "quiet Asian boys." *Anthropology and Education Quarterly, 42*(2), 158–181.

Lorde, A. (1983). *Sister outsider.* Freedom, CA: The Crossing Press.

McKittrick, K. (2006). *Demonic grounds: Black women and the cartographies of struggle.* Minneapolis: University of Minnesota Press.

Moraga, C., & Anzaldua, G. (Eds.). (1983). *This bridge called my back.* Berkeley, CA: Third Woman Press.

Morris, E.W. (2007). "Ladies" or "loudies"? Perceptions and experiences of black girls in classrooms. *Youth & Society, 38*(4), 490–515.

Pillow, W. (2004). *Unfit subjects: Educational policy and the teen mother.* New York: RoutledgeFalmer.

Scott, J. (2001). Watching me. On *Who Is Jill Scott: Words and Sounds, vol. 1* [recording]. California: Hidden Beach Recording.

Shange, N. (1975). *For colored girls who have considered suicide when the rainbow is enuf.* New York: Macmillan.

Shujaa, M.J. (1998). *Too much schooling, too little education: A paradox of black life in white societies.* Trenton, NJ: Africa World Press, Inc.

Weems, M.E. (2003). *Public education and the imagination-intellect: I speak from the wound in my mouth.* New York: Peter Lang.

Zita, J.N. (1998). *Body talk: Philosophical reflections on sex and gender.* New York: Columbia University Press.

ꜱfiveꜱ

The Kindness of [Medical] Strangers

An Ethnopoetic Account of Embodiment, Empathy, and Engagement

Elyse Pineau

I've always depended on the kindness of strangers.[1] No stranger to the medical industries in both the United States and Canada, I have spent countless days and weeks and months in hospital rooms, operating rooms, waiting rooms, and administrative corridors. In the pursuit of my own and my family members' care, I've run gauntlets of surgeons, social workers, and rotating staff who are always new strangers, because they've just come on at the shift change and haven't the time to steal from the hospital schedule to sit with a patient and call them by name. "What choice do we have?" they might rightfully ask. "There's a whole long hallway of vital statistics to take, and it's our job and it's vital, this data we gather." Their point is well taken: the efficiency of Western medicine depends on strict schedules and emotional and bodily detachment. Consider the ritual of medical rounds: gloved fingers on pulse, eyes on watch, pen on paper, like an ironic sacrament of reverse transubstantiation where Flesh becomes Word graphed on the chart at the end of your bed. Yet these coded communiqués, however vital they are, obscure the fact that no amount of text can ever bear the weight of the bodies they stand in for (Pineau, 2000).

Over the years I have become painfully familiar, for example, with the perfunctory intimacy of overworked aides performing routine hygiene procedures on bodies too physically or mentally compromised to resist, to insist they be looked in the eye and called by name—that most perfunctory of human courtesies—whenever a perfect stranger strips them naked and puts hands on their bodies. In the performance[2] of *Nursing Mother* I have called you out: "Robin, Mary, Ellen, Sue, Bob, Nancy, Francis!" When I was called to play patient's advocate, tilting at insurance corporations, blue cross on my shield, I've taken names—"Tom, Dick, & Harry!" When you played me for a chump in the contractual fine print that turns health coverage into windmills, spinning out of reach with the slightest breeze from the wave of an underwriter's pen. So believe me when I tell you that I am no stranger to the machines of medical science or the machinations of profit-based, corporatized health care.

From this backlog of embodied knowledge and through a method of performative inquiry, I've come to believe that depending on the kindness of strangers is the foundational paradox of a health care model whose reliance on biotechnology and the economics that sustain it, depends upon institutionalizing bodily estrangement in order to work its medical miracles. As an autoethnographic performance poet, I have built a body of work that critiques the medicalized female body across the life span of women's health care. Reflecting back on that work, I'll own up to a certain lack of kindness in the pleasure I have taken when I can craft a critical insight into a clever rhythmic phrase that publicly skewers all those cocky docs and their docky cocks—double-troping patriarchy to show that kindness and dependence make strange bedfellows when differently valued bodies are placed in the service of science, in the pursuit of a profit, and in the reproduction of race, class, & gender relations.

And yet I am no stranger to kindness. Over years of procedures, I have been transfigured by moments of authentic presence, deep compassion, and embodied empathy from medical personnel who were committed to a practice of care giving that is grounded in the fundamental dignity of each human being and the healing power of human touch. An engaged social conscience begins by acknowledging the standpoint and self-determination of all whom we engage, especially within the relational dynamics of our research (Spry, 2006; Madison, 2006). I realize, with the clarity of critical hindsight, that I have done an injustice to those kind strangers in whose care I have been healed and wholed. I have turned them into tropes and targets to serve my critique of a system in which they, too, labor as best they can. How much more accurate and ethically complex it seems now, to highlight their small acts of kindness, their own small acts of resistance against the institutional protocols that constrained us all.

Accordingly, I use this essay to effect a double resistance. First, by restoring and representing the compassionate acts of my caregivers, I reveal the myriad, mundane ruptures in the medical system effected by a genuine and humane praxis of care. Second, I call attention to the ethical responsibilities of the artist-advocate to the communities she renders in writing by replacing a rhetoric of opposition with one of alliance and mutuality. Commensurate with Weems's (2003) elaboration of "the imagination intellect" as a means to revision and reinvent social realities, I use poetic narrative to reexamine and revalue the quality of care that is possible, despite institutional and situational constraints. What follows, then, is a series of counter narratives—kinder narratives if you will—organized around the litany of names through which I have previously excoriated them. "Robin, Mary, Ellen, Sue, Bob, Nancy, Francis, Tom, Dick, & Harry," I offer you now a self-correcting discourse about the times when the kindness of strangers was all I could depend upon.

Robin

It had been 17 years since I last heard her voice, but I recognized the sound in an instant, over my shoulder in the checkout line at the local food Co-Op one day this spring. Turning around, I saw that she held a basket overflowing with fresh produce while the other rested lightly & proprietarily on the mounded belly of a young woman beside her whose resemblance left no doubt about kinship. "Robin?" I asked. "Elyse!" she exclaimed. And without hesitation, she swept me up in her arms right there in that public checkout line and hugged me so hard and so long, you would have thought we were kin.

Backstory: Robin had been the hospital childbirth educator the year that my son was born. She had coached us through 6 months of preparation for a "natural" childbirth, and later she was the one who prepared my body for the C-section and kept hold of my hand the whole time I was wheeled down the hall on my gurney to the room with the knives. It was Robin's voice I latched onto, coming out of the surgical fog with a gash in my belly and a baby to care for.

Backstory: In the first 24 hours following abdominal surgery, every movement is excruciating, engaging as it does the core abdominal muscles that have just been sliced and sewn back together. Compound this bodily rupture with the onset of lactation, the fugue-states of pain medication, and the urgent rooting of a wriggling newborn, the weight of whose need so clearly exceeds the scope of the manuals you've studied while you waited to hold him—as if nursing came naturally, without the bodied knowledge of rehearsal. And so for 24 hours, I had lain flat on my back with a foot of sutures holding my insides in, unschooled and unable to position my own or my infant's body for nursing.

And my son had an appetite. The nurses had nicknamed him "the snapping turtle" because when they brought him in to me, each hour on the hour, he would snake out his head and clamp down so hard on my flesh that he raised welts and blood blisters with each attempt to latch on. With each shift change that first day, a new entourage of strange on-call nurses & residents would peek their heads in to survey the damage and prescribe "icepacks" or "pain meds," depending upon their predilection for palliation. "You'll get the hang of it," they assured me airily; "it's quite natural to feel some routine discomfort when you're a new mother, nursing."

And then they would sweep out of my room on rounds, leaving a howling and hungry infant draped across my wounded belly and bloodied breasts.

By the time Robin arrived—"just checking in on my new mothers," she chirped—I was desperate with pain and deeply shamed by my failure to perform this most routine maternal procedure. "Well, this is nonsense!" she said and *without a moment's hesitation*, she climbed right up on my bed beside me, spooning her body around mine, one arm wrapped round my belly to cradle his body against mine and mine against hers, teaching me, body to body, the secret to holding him so that milk would flow and he could nurse without drawing blood. Looking back, I like to imagine us like those Russian nesting dolls—*matrushka*—all spooned together in that hospital bed, while a generational wisdom passed from body to body through a full-bodied and unconditional *praxis of care*. Robin froze time in that moment. The intimacy of touch demands the luxury of time, and Robin dared to steal time back from institutionalized protocols, where new mothers are routinely checked in and checked out without benefit of learning how bodies can nestle for comfort and for nurture. I carry the sense memory of Robin's embrace deep in my cells; it is a *felt sense of presence,* like a generational wisdom about the importance of authentic engagement and *empowerment* through embodied empathy.

And standing in the Co-Op checkout line this spring hugging Robin tight, belly to belly, we both remembered that moment when kindness and compassion had made kin of strangers.

Mary, Ellen, Sue, Bob, and Nancy

I won't pretend that these were their actual names because they genuinely were strangers. I may have met them only once in the comings and goings of shift changes and rounds and routine staff replacements, yet their actions are indelible in my memory. Was it "Mary" whom I watched close my mother's eyes and wash my mother's face with such tenderness and dignity as I stood in the doorway, 4 minutes late to witness her passing? Was "Ellen" the name of the aide who used to sneak us orange sherbet from the nurse's station when we discovered that it was the only thing that could trick Mom into swallowing her pills instead of spitting them out? And I'll never forget (we'll call her) "Sue" as she gripped my hands and held my gaze, tears welling in her own eyes, while a perky, pony-tailed med student who was half our ages, blithely & without preamble, turned her back on me to probe the sutures in my belly and pronounce me infected. I'm almost certain that "Bob" was the name of the personal assistant who waited in line for an hour to pay his respects at Dad's funeral, although it was his only day off from the nursing home's schedule, and I will always be grateful that "Nancy" volunteered her overtime to stand in for the surgical nurse on my second C-section because she thought that I might need to see a familiar face among the strangers gathered at my table to cut me.

Memories cast narrative coherence retrospectively over the shoulder of experience. I evoke "Mary, Ellen, Sue, Bob, and Nancy" as composite characters gleaned from a long string of small acts of kindness scattered frequently and often spontaneously along the hospital corridors of my memory. Each name is a reminder that in the briefest gesture of compassion, the most mundane *performative of care*—a smile, a hand held, an ally made, a sacrifice of time, a courtesy given, a dignity restored—lies the power to crack open and resignify the meaning and power of "hands-on care." "Mary, Ellen, Sue, Bob, and Nancy": I write you to stand in for all the others who've stood against the system and disrupted, derailed, and dismantled, however fleetingly, the machinery of medical detachment. Compassion is compassion is compassion, and by any other name, the memory of those profoundly humanizing gestures from a string of strangers would still be as sweet.

Francis

Surgeons are not known for their bedside manner, and yet when he stood at the side of my bed in the operating room as they prepped me for the spinal block, it was his manner I remember, although I've failed, until now, to recount it in any story I've told about my daughter's birth.

Backstory: It is standard procedure when administering a spinal that the patient sit on the edge of the operating table and slowly curve his or her body forward to expose each node of the spine to the anesthetist's needle. This strange man—because statistically speaking it generally is—then fingers you from behind, finding just the right spot in your vertebrae where needle penetration will produce the desired effect: the encroachment of non-sensation that signals your body is ready for entry. The puncture itself doesn't hurt, really—its just a little prick, after all—and yet the sensation it produces is profoundly disorienting, as numbness creeps from your toes to your hips to your breath until your body is entirely dislocated from itself, awake and aware, but unable to feel that awareness in any material way. It is, for me, an ontological disjunct, and Francis knew this and took compassion on me.

Positioning his body directly in front of mine, he let me lean in and rest my forehead on his shoulder as if to say "borrow the solidity of my body; it will help you sustain a sense of your own." Now, it could be that this leaning is routine procedure in operating rooms to ensure that the patient doesn't just tip over off the table, but I think there was more to it than that. As paralysis progressed and my panic rose, I turned my head sideways, burrowing closer against his neck— you know the way you do, sometimes, when a man holds you and your face fits right into that liminal space between the pulse in his neck and the breadth of his shoulders? I felt his body stiffen for a second, for surely the strange intimacy of this touch breached guidelines that govern the manner in which the bodies of surgeons engage with those of their patients. But then he softened. He placed his hand—his surgical hand—gently on the side of my face and held it there, as if to say: "Hush now; I've got you and I will not let you fall." And I felt my own body soften and yield, surrendering control to the assurance that my powerless self was, indeed, in "good hands."

And I don't know why I've never told that moment of the story before in any staged or scholarly recounting. On the one hand, it did not support the argument about bodily estrangement on which I've built my critiques of women's health care. But neither does its inclusion, now, undercut the overarching truth of that case. Perhaps I intuitively elided this part of the story in crafting *Nursing Mother* because my poet-performer's ear knew it would not serve the accelerating rhythm and abrupt scene montages I was using to make my argument, both dramatically and rhetorically. But no accounting is innocent, and claims to partiality or contingency and even rhetorical efficacy feel insufficient from the vantage point of ten years' reflection on the representational tensions and muddy moral quandaries that attend autoethnographic work.

Still, my erasure of Francis's gesture in that operating room needles my conscience, calling me back for a second look, a self-critical re-examination of the moments I've glossed in the service of a broader critical agenda. The confession is no mere scholarly handwringing, a superficial and self-serving nod to the perspectival contingencies that attend scholarship in general and autoethnographic work in particular. I've come to believe it is ethically insufficient to say "I could not see it then" if I do not assume the labor of "seeing it now" from the vantage point of a more seasoned personal and professional standpoint. Critical reflexivity is the hallmark of qualitative inquiry; it demands an epistemological commitment to "think on one's thinking" and the limits of knowledge one can produce in any particular moment. Puzzling through the evolutionary nature of autoethnographic insight, I turned to a colleague, Craig Gingrich-Phillbrook, whose work likewise cycles back on itself in pursuit of more nuanced self-other narrations. Drawing on Levinas's notion of alterity as commanded by the face of the other, Craig theorized:

> A protentional (Levinasian) ethics would remind us that we still must face (i.e., come face to face with) the others whom we represent, if not literally then in our conscience, in the cosmos, in the great quantum unknown. And the thing is, that relation changes over time, so we may regret what we said and/or what we did not say about them. In such cases, I think it's our protentional obligation to "follow up" the piece, to show the evolution of the record, more than "set it straight," which I do not believe can ever happen, ontologically. (personal correspondence, 2011)

I return, then, to "the scene of the crime" of erasure, not with the hubris of setting the record straight, but rather with the humility of recognizing the humanity my previous stories have stolen.

Tom, Dick, & Harry

They are such easy targets, those boys. I've taken my share of potshots at them and justifiably so, for the colloquialism crystallizes the faceless anonymity that is the mainstay of biotechnology and profit-based health care. But they are not anonymous, these servants of a system that curtails from the outset their ability to be humane because it is not time efficient, or financially feasible, or even part of their medical training. So whose systematic depersonalization is at play here when I make "Tom, Dick, & Harry" a metonym for all that is wrong with an industry that stands in for their bodies as surely as it does for my own. Such erasure of their personhood is not only unkind, it is uncritical. Who am I to claim that they do not recognize my body when they are the ones who've bathed it, drawn its blood, bound up its wounds, and washed its shit. It is the bloody body, after all, that calls the Samaritan, and when I have been laid low at the side of the road, Tom, Dick, & Harry did not pass me by. I have depended on their kindness, these medical strangers. They have been my body's keepers. It is time, then, that I return their kindness, by returning their bodies to the story…for safekeeping.

Notes

1. In troping Blanche Dubois's plaintive abjection in Tennessee Williams's *A Streetcar Named Desire,* I want to evoke the closing scene and the genuine kindness—tenderness even—with which those medical strangers escorted her wounded body to the ambulance. As a concept, "kindness" is always complicated, conflictual, contextualized; as a concrete embodied action, such as those I narrate in this essay, it is no less than a transformative praxis of engaged empathy.
2. Taking up the challenge of a critical turn on my own scholarship, I have woven into this essay many of the arguments and poetic phrasing deployed in my earlier work, particularly *Nursing Mother.*

References

Gingrich-Phillbrook, C. (2011). A protentional ethics [personal email correspondence]. Retrieved January 27, 2012.

Madison, D.S. (2006). The dialogic performative in critical ethnography. *Text and Performance Quarterly, 26*(4), 320–324.

Pineau, E.L. (2000). "Nursing mother" and articulating absence. *Text and Performance Quarterly, 20*(1), 1–19.

Spry, T. (2006). A "performative-I" copresence: Embodying the ethnographic turn in performance and the performative turn in ethnography." *Text and Performance Quarterly, 26*(4), 339–346.

Weems, M.E. (2003). *Public education and the imagination-intellect: I speak from the wound in my mouth.* New York: Peter Lang.

The Poetics of Black Mother-Womanhood

Amira Davis

I am a mother, grand and even greatly grand. I am raced, gendered, and classed, ever so tendentiously, in the middle. These markers, some self-determined, some overly determined, are the ways in which and by which I identify and am identified. My form and voice signal a social location that introduces me to a wider audience who bring to the marketplace encounter their composite identities. The marketplace is where consumables are valued, traded, dickered over, and negotiations made. Relations are fluid and forming. Associations are either harmonic or dissonant, but never neutral. Mediated by socially and culturally constructed conceptualizations of human existence formed and reformed within hegemonic worldviews, my inner self is reified through my external markers—what it means to be female, Black, and re/productive: meanings that are communicated before I speak my understanding of who I am.

Bio
I am 9 months of Bettye's sorrow & joy
the pride and fear of my father, Lamar
I am the aspirations of George & Carrie
the longings of Millie and Ed,
the desires of Fannie, Julia, Richard, John & Vinnie
this is my ancestral line tracing back
to another time

Before I was shaped & honed
by whips, words, nooses
& raped mothers

Before melaninated
flesh weighted me
like coffle chains
strangling my bones

Before strife and struggle
defined me
to a time before
I was raced and erased
gendered, classed, located, situated,
nothing-ed and othered

Before posting up at the crossroads
Elegba, O!
postmoderned/
post-raced/
post-feminist/
posthuman

I return to the center
to recover, repair, & renew
to reach back
to Sankofa
Se wo were finawosankofaayinke
It is not taboo to go back & fetch what has been lost, stolen or forgotten
Se wo were finawosankofaayinke
It is not taboo to go back & fetch what has been lost, stolen or forgotten
Se wo were finawosankofaayinke
It is not taboo to go back & fetch what has been lost, stolen or forgotten

Back before the time,
before the time,
before the time

I extend forward like Nut[1]
through the lives of my children
Their children and those yet unborn
They who will re-member me
And chant my name
And chant my name

And chant my name

I am Bettye's nine month sorrowing joy
The pride & fear of my father, Lamar
I am the aspirations of George & Carrie
The longings of Millie and Ed,
The desires of Fannie, Julia, Richard, John & Vinnie
The scion of rememorying seed

I am the greatness of a grand mother
who stood on the banks of the Cassamance
the smell of juicy melons & tall grass
under a gray-blue night
a lover ripe and fresh
she licks the taste from his lips
and births my life

On Being Raced, Gendered, Judged, and Adjudicated

Under the violence of patriarchal, white racial superiority, to be Black and female, classed and colored has resulted in them, as an overdetermined group, to be situated at the bottom of the social scale. Jason Richwine, a National Research Initiative fellow at the American Enterprise Institute who completed a dissertation on immigration and IQ at Harvard University's Kennedy School of Government, has identified an intellectual hierarchy in the United States that places Blacks at the bottom of a scale that is topped by Jews and Asians, Anglo-Americans, and then Latinos (American Enterprise Institute, 2008). As the female of any group is lower than the male, Black women are at the absolute bottom. The constant reiteration of inferiority and the devaluation of human worth based on Eurocentric values and markers of advancement and civilization perpetuate the victimization and alienation of Black women. High-status, assimilated African American women have been unable to escape the chains of Mammy, Sapphire, and Jezebel. Ugly, loud, angry, hypersexual, hypercritical, neglectful, and amoral are but a few characterizations of Black womanhood.

Flapjacks

I am fat, jet black/with ruby red cheeks
short tufts of nappy kinks/hide under my kerchief
I can carry the full weight of Marsa'/firmly on top my head
while my babies trot behind/barefoot, naked, & neglected
clinging to the tail/of my linsey-woolsey dress
I made flapjacks a hot commodity/

a woman you wouldn't dream of bedding
unless you were into mother-fucking
made famous by my sheer/ridiculousness
…who am i?

Jezebel
From out of the Lake
this Jezebel strode,
crafted and drafted
on notepaper and travelogues
sexualized/mythologized

I heard grown men call for god
from between their teeth
when the rhythm rocked her hips
and the beads of sweat formed
on her breasts
rolled down and settled
in the small of her back
I heard them moan out loud
scorched by the heat
of her thighs touching themselves
their hands pressed against
cowhide skin drums
like spanking warm flesh

I heard them declare, "Lord have mercy!"

The Preacher man called her the bastard child of evil
the devil deceiver
the manipulator, controller
the soul stealer
immortalized in twizzle stick holders
and Black memorabilia/with nutcracker thighs[2]

she dripped baptismal
waters on his altar
bounced her flesh under his nose
he grabbed his loins
slapped his bible
and screamed out "Oh, my lawd"
I heard him shout
Sweet Jeezus

Black Women and the Power of the Word (Ọ̀rọ̀): Methodology

I self-identify as a Black woman, consistent with the markers that signal to others "who" I am, reified by skin, pigment, and the contours of my human form. I am also mind and spirit. I exist beyond the visual gaze, where I am apprehended by the interpretation of my voice, imagined through my textual self and my self-proclamations that, of necessity, are only partial self-disclosures. These are the betrayals of the written text. The reader and the writer meet at a borderline with rich, deep, and ancient spaces on either side. Inasmuch as these encounters are fraught with tension, they create the opportunity for mutually transformative possibilities for the creation of higher, r/evolutionary understanding.

From the perspective of the Yoruba of Southwestern Nigeria, a culture that has left an indelible mark on the culture of the Americas due to the large numbers of Yoruba transported to the New World during the Transatlantic Slave Trade (TAST) (Iliffe, 1995), the word has power (Washington, 2005). Teresa N. Washington (2005), an African American priestess initiated into the Yoruba system and an independent scholar, tells us that "Ọ̀rọ̀ (power of the word), manifests itself in many ways, including ọfọ̀ase (the power to pray effectively), àyàjo (power of incantations), and adásàn (the power to curse and drive insane)" (p. 17). According to the Odu Ifa, the sacred text of the Yoruba, women develop these oracular powers as a result of menstruation.

Black women writers, artists, poets, visual artists, dancers, musicians, and cultural workers whose ontological and epistemological frameworks are informed by the broader collective identity of what it means to be Black and female inside of Western culture seek to reclaim and resurrect the public persona of Black woman/motherhood, using tools that they create and define from. It is through their oracular utterances that they "create ritual dramas, proverbs, divination texts, healing rituals, and other forms of artistic and spiritual expression, including contemporary literature, music, and visual arts." These cultural productions "honor the Mother's original utterance and sustain, flavor, and structure society" (Washington, 2005, p. 17).

Womanwork: A Story of Black Women's Labor
One day
Husband takes Wife
from the village
Wife leaves behind
Her home & family
The earth she once tilled
upon her back Baby rides like a saddle

Wife is the bearer of future plans

Together they hunger
eating sparingly of the dried plantains & cowpeas
Wife secrets away for security

Together they walk
from sun to moon & moon to sun
finally arriving at the forest's edge
a lush carpet of pearl millet
stretches before them
running to the water's edge
they discern the sweet scent of wet earth and dung

It is here the bush cows graze

Wife looks to her Husband
and re-sees a long line of *kijana*[3]
walking from the clearing towards the sacred grove
their silhouettes cast upon the horizon
they will return with cut penises & heroic tales
as *wanaume*[4]

Her stomach growls in anticipation

Husband looks to Wife
recalling stories of elder *wanawake,*[5]
possessors of plant knowledge of leaves
forest knowers who apprentice *wasichana*[6]
in the power of menstrual blood

Husband whispers to Wife
"Dear Wife. I hear that you possess some little magic... please, use it to capture one of the bush cows, that I may/we may have something to eat and not perish."
"Husband," Wife responds in disbelief. *"Do you mean what you ask..?"*
"I mean it," says Husband.

With reservation
she loosens the fabric
that adheres Baby to her back
she unknots the string tie of her lappa
it falls to the earth
exposing her feminine form

Beads that graced her small waist
and ample flanks
trickle to the ground

circling her calloused feet

Her eyes narrow to squinting
Her pupils dilate, irises yellow
she crouches low
hair springs like sorghum
from skin once smooth
three inch fangs, like sharpened tusks
sprout from her once warm smile

In fright Husband retreats
leaving *mtoto* [7] in the instant
torn between awe & fear

Wife moves stealth-like through the grasses
until she comes within striking distance of the herd
she lays low, awaiting her moment
then with the power in her haunches
Wife springs forward
and before panic could register
she leaps upon Bush Cow's back

With the muscle of her jaws
and the force of her feral form
she brings the bush cow down
in one quick
linear motion without break
without pause

Once done
woman turns her gaze to the place
where Husband last stood
she scans the dark spaces
between tree trunks & foliage
finally spying him
perched among the branches

She drags Bush Cow across the expanse
depositing her prey
at the place of Husband's refuge
with a thirsty tongue
she laps jugular blood from her teeth

At its taste, she returns

claws retract, hair retreats
her muscular buttocks reform
her breasts hang like ripe melons
from her chest
she comes erect
once again Wife and Mother
she scoops and cradles Baby

Husband descends slowly
down the tree's trunk
his mouth spilling over with platitudes
for his young wife,
the mother of his child

"Wife, you were magnificent, so majestic. I knew I chose well my bride. Now we will eat and not starve."

In the back of his mind
he wonders
can he ever trust her again

Moral of the story: *"Never ask a woman to do a man's work…"*

Border Crossings: Theorizing the Empathic Other

…the relationship between the mundane, everyday sociocultural processes and cultural performances is not unidirectional and "positive"—in the sense that the performative genre merely "reflects" or "expresses" the social system or the cultural configuration, or at any rate their key relationships—but that it is reciprocal and reflexive—in the sense that the performance is often a critique, direct or veiled, of the social life it grows out of, an evaluation (with lively possibilities of reject) of the way society handles history. (Performance theorist Victor Turner on the pedagogical possibilities of performance, 1986, p. 22)

Cultural performances provide the opportunity for collective community transcendence as rituals that are part of the ongoing social process where people "become conscious, through witnessing and often participating" in the performance. By doing so participants discover the "nature, texture, style, and given meanings of their own lives as members of a sociocultural community" (Turner, 1986, p. 22). In this context, Turner goes further to say that

cultural performances are not simple reflectors or expressions of culture or even of changing culture but may themselves be active agencies of change, representing the eye by which culture sees itself and the drawing board on which creative actors sketch out what they believe to be more apt or interesting designs for living. (p. 24)

It is in the space of the cultural performance, orally, aurally, textually, and/ or visually that empathy is either created or abandoned. There are no guarantees mediated as these encounters are by partial truths, distrust, stereotypes, and grand narratives. Black women's cultural work cuts against the grain of whiteness and masculinity, performing resistance, protest, realities, and aspirations. It speaks back to power in ways potentially compelling the audience to solidarity, or guilting them into paralysis or regenerate feelings of total repulsion (Sonnega, 2001). These are the risks and challenges in exposing one's vulnerability in the hopes of building bridges and mutual humanity.

A Matter of Time
In another time
I arrived here
in chains, unfree,
spoken in extremes

too Black, too loud, too strong, too fertile, too easy, too diseased

forced across seas,
beyond reason, into madness
my voice not lost
but stolen
a Baobab tree
etched into my remembering back
with whips branches tipped
with budding, bloody leaves;
deep roots that span two worlds

400 years have passed
& I have not yet learned to navigate
the hyphened space
between the African & the American
me
 but who counts the seasons?

Ma Rainey sang her blues for me
like Bessie did, and Billie
crooned Strange Fruit
while Zora told of eyes
that watched for gods

My mothers: grand, great and just
were blues women, too
sensuality & soul sifted through ancestral sounds
low moans birthed in cramped quarters
a battle cry to Warrior spirits named
Oya, Hatshepsut, Nzingha
Granny Nanny, Mother Harriet,
Asanteyaa, Ella, Fannie Lou, Queen Mother Moore,
Vina & Bettye Melba
It is the song of black birds
perched atop trees
bearing witness
In the timbre of their tune I hear the question asked,
"How long?"
Response: Not long.

I channel these mother tongues on stages
in meetings, in classrooms, on pages
in languages of resource & policy
in places sacred & profane
my scream reverberates from inner
to outer and cyber space
biting words rush from my mind like
self-emancipated slaves
they burn my lips, my fingertips
unmasking my invisibility
leaving people to wonder,
 "Why is she so angry?!"
Do you not see arms that ache
for babies lost and stolen?
sold in marketplaces, on auction blocks,
to private prisons and for-profit care,
killed in imperial & urban wars
poetic tragedies in which Kiyanna, Kiwane
Larry and Boo forever die
on city streets
denied the right to live
safe & whole

I mourn memories,
collective & private
wombs: cut off/cut out

after birthing & wet-nursing america
to her magnificent
the massive breasts of the state now dry
sag around her bloated middle
the true mark of an old vulture

Perhaps my anger reflects
the tiredness of my pain

Chants of democracy
lose meaning in survival struggle
that consumes each new thought in utero,
necrotizes the flesh from action

before my eyes,
in 24 hour news cycles
voters become voteless
the landed made landless
the once housed now homeless
unruly markets shape shift
into tsunamis
& the price of food soars like eagles

In these crowded corners
superbugs named MRSA[8] rival
HIV/AIDS as new parasites
in hosting Black bodies
where rats & roaches feed
alongside politicians & money changers
who violate the body of We The People
& are bailed out with its life blood through
gas pump hoses
and credit card debt

Where once feared street thugs called GDs[9]
are now called G8s & G20s
and while the golden arches
may sometime resemble an oasis
in the expanse of food deserts
I can't rescue my kids with
"happy" meals

Overwhelmed with jingoism
the margins are filled with those

who consume the goods of life
with foreign trademarks
their our own shelf life
less than in 3rd world nations

I stand here
not alone, but with the ghosts
of mothers/sisters/aunts/nieces/daughters
crowding my space,
speaking through bodies, real
and incorporeal

We gather here to commiserate,
cleanse ourselves with prayer,
clinging to holy water amulets
bathed in tears
the brazen among us
push tight clenched fists
into the face of the center
and swear our oath of r/evolution
this poem our offering to life
& light/hope & healing,
peace, love & the desire
to draw breath
one day again
free

I heard in his question, "How long 'til freedom?"
Call: How long? Response: Not long
but tell me, who really counts the seasons?

Conclusion: The Circularity of Return

As Freire (1970/2000) informs us, we are all unfinished beings, humans in the process of becoming. Our stories have the power to transform, disrupt, give new meanings and generate better understandings, internally and externally. The performance of Black woman/motherhood is structured by race, class, sexuality, geography, and other factors that serve as the prism through which those elements constitutive of Blackness, femaleness, and reproducing bodies are viewed. Into this refractive glare, my stories are performed and told, as catharsis, monologue, and dialog. I use words to speak out loud my personal truth that connects historically, politically, culturally and socially to a larger body of stories and truths. My aim is to aid the many and multiple Black woman/mother stories in their richness and complexity. These endeavors are grounded in a concept known among the Yoruba as Ìfọgbọ́ntáayése, meaning literally, "using wisdom to remake/improve the world" (Lawal, 1996). Ase! Ase! Ase!

Notes

1. Nut is the sky goddess of ancient Egypt/Kemet
2. Nude Black women were featured as novelty items such as drink stirrers and nutcrackers. These items are now sold as Black memorabilia of unknown dates. The nutcrackers were made of wood with a hinge that enabled the legs to open. A nut was placed in the crouch and the legs would be brought together, crushing the nut.
3. Swahili word for initiates
4. Swahili word for men
5. Swahili word for women
6. Swahili word for adolescent girls
7. Swahili word for baby
8. Methicillin-resistant Staphylococcus aureus (MRSA) is a type (strain) of staph bacteria that does not respond to some antibiotics that are commonly used to treat staph infections.
9. Gangster Disciples or Black Gangster Disciples are an African-American street gang that was founded on the South Side of Chicago in the late 1960s. The gang is known for proliferating drugs and violence.

References

American Enterprise Institute. (2008, July 1). The new case against immigration. Available at http://www.aei.org/video/100934

Freire, P. (2000). *Pedagogy of the oppressed* (30th anniversary ed.). New York: Continuum.

Iliffe, J. 1995. *Africans: The history of a continent*. New York: Cambridge University Press.

Lawal, B. (1996). *The Gẹ̀lẹ̀dẹ́ spectacle: Art, gender, and social harmony in an African culture*. Seattle: University of Washington Press.

Sonnega, W. (2001). Beyond a liberal audience. In H.J, Elam, Jr., & D. Krasner (Eds.), *African American performance and theater history: A critical reader* (pp. 81–98). New York: Oxford University Press.

Turner, V. 1986. *The anthropology of performance*. New York: PAJ Publications.

Washington, T.N. (2005). *Our mothers, our powers, our texts: Manifestations of Àjẹ́ in Africana literature*. Bloomington: Indiana University Press.

Seven

Stop in the Name of

An Auto/ethnographic Response to Violence Against Black Women [1]

Mary E. Weems

The results of woman-hating in the Black community are tragedies which diminish all Black people. These acts must be seen in the context of a systematic devaluation of Black women within this society. It is within this context that we become approved and acceptable targets for Black male rage.
—Lorde, 1984, p. 65

I continue to use writing as my method (Richardson, 1994). I've lived through domestic violence. While I often challenge myself, friends, colleagues, students, and others to write as acts against injustice, as one way of beginning to heal and of helping others as they engage the work, I haven't wanted to publicly face the reality of my own vulnerability to loving the wrong men, men with their own mental and emotional issues, men incapable of love because they didn't love themselves, abusive men. Media reports about the murder of two local professional Black women I didn't know, coupled with the murder a few years earlier of another one of my young relatives, pushed me to write.

Loneliness is a helluva drug. I met him in the middle of mama's friend's dining room, one smile and a few compliments all it took to get my phone number, a phone call all it took for a first date, the heroin tattoos up both arms handled with a deep French kiss and *Jody's* promise that addiction was in his past. After a few months I invited him to move in; I played Etta James singing "At Last" in the background. Our 2-year relationship was a series of short honeymoons, as he travelled in and out of town hauling steel on eighteen wheels. Friday, when he came home, was the best day of the week, Sunday, a cozy breakfast in the morning before he got back on the road. One year later. My daughter missed a father, I was in what I thought was love. I asked him to marry me. We married at the courthouse—no dress, no flowers, no rings, no honeymoon.

Jody changed as if a switch in him cut on. He started coming home less often on the weekends, stopped calling while he was on the road, stopped being as intimate. I thought *What's wrong with me? Why doesn't he love me? If I just love him enough he'll change back to the man I wanted to marry.* The first time, he was home during the week. A girlfriend dropped by and we were in the kitchen laughing and talking. He called me into the bathroom off the kitchen. I'm suddenly scared, not of what he'll do—that my friend will hear us. *Jody* accuses me of stealing money from pockets that came home empty. When I open my red mouth to call him a liar, he punches me in the stomach and grins. Doubled over, I bite my tongue, he opens the door enough to get out, says goodnight to my friend, leaves shutting the back door off the kitchen quietly behind him. I'm on the toilet seat making myself say *I'll be out in a minute* as if I'm okay. When I come out, her face is shaped in the polite stare of a woman who's been there too. She makes an excuse to leave, hugs me, not too close.

I don't hear from *Jody* for days. Too proud to tell anyone, I take care of my little girl who keeps looking at me with love and questions—I feel like the child, wonder why he's acting like this, wonder what I've done, wonder how to stop it from happening again. It's Friday. He comes home tired, hungry, and gentle. I am bathed, oiled, perfumed. His apology is long and hard. I'm happy until Sunday. Convinced when he says it won't happen again. It does. A few weeks later, he accuses me of stealing his paycheck. I'm trying to explain that he must have misplaced it. He's not hearing me. Glad my daughter's not home, I try to fight back. His gun in my hand holds him back until he snatches the folding bedroom door from its frame, hits me in the mouth, I drop the gun. Screaming, I spread my blood on the walls, break dishes, glasses, chairs, while he watches.

Later, his voice soothes, he convinces me to calm down, asks me why I made him angry, and asks me if I still love him. He helps me to the bathroom, my face in the mirror: blood on the left side of my mouth from a gash that needs stitches. He never hits me where it will show—how does he know? Later, he takes me to the emergency room, explains an accident to the nurse, waits for me, the loving husband, takes me home, bathes me, makes what I believe is love. Next, morning the mess I made waits for me to clean it up—he watches. I do.

Two years later, I walk around wearing the same jeans, tennis shoes, scarves on my head. Mama tries to help—I think she's trying to break us up. I feel dazed, half empty. Holding on to my second marriage, not wanting to be a failure, not wanting to put my daughter through losing another man she still loves like a daddy. He is using and worse. I hear rumors from other truckers about crack pipes, needles, alcohol. I turn inside out like an old t-shirt, keep trying to become the woman he fell in love with, keep trying to find a way to love him enough to change him. Granny says leave him, that a man don't change nothin' but his clothes—but I didn't know what that meant. Finally I got tired. One Friday, he comes home and I tell him to get out, that I don't want him in my house any more. I think I'm ready for anything. I'm not. He grabs my daughter, takes her out of the house, and keeps her in his car all night. Next morning his son who lives on the third floor lets them in while I'm sleeping. I tell my daughter to stay in her room. [*I don't remember everything—memory in pieces like the broken plates.*] He drags me down the steps, somehow I break free, run upstairs, lock him and his son out.

Weeks and weeks blur—late night phone calls, mama's unasked for advice, my daughter's confusion—the look on her face when I let her out of her room. He's cleaned out our bank account. I have to get a job—from 33K with GM to $6.50 an hour. I have to wait for my first pay to buy a pair of stockings. Weeks pass. I hear he's sleeping with his son on a couch at one of my male relative's house—he's telling a story—my relative's listening. Finally, he gets me on the phone by calling from an unknown number. He begs to come back, tells me he loves me, asks forgiveness, asks for a single shoe he says he left under my bed. I say if you ever call me again, I'm going to prosecute you for domestic violence and child endangering. He leaves me and the shoe alone.

Ruth used to tell me stories in the basement—her part of the house. We were surrounded by soldiers. Tall bottles of cheap gin, standing like invisible guards until the day she died, when her husband's friends dragged them from the basement by the dozens for over an hour. A coffee cup drinker told me she never put the liquor bottles out cause she didn't want the garbage men to know how much she drank. A beauty inside and out, when she was young, Elizabeth Taylor could have looked like her if she were light skinned and Black. Connected by love, she was like another mother. I kept her secrets like a child afraid the boogey man would come and steal her away if I told. Married at fifteen, her mother thought she was set for life. Her life: Dropped out of high school for the only man she ever loved, kept in the house like a pet, obedient cat, let out to shop and take care of a business he claimed that was in her name.

Her tales were full of him. Making his pajamas by hand, keeping his clothes pristine, manicures, pedicures, cleaning, pressing, waiting, waiting, waiting for him to come home—always drunk, always late at night, always another woman's smell on his clothes. He liked to take the world out on her, his fists golden gloves in her face, her eyes black and blue one year for Thanksgiving, the meal she prepared covering the kitchen—all his favorites waiting for company that didn't come. Hard to believe but true, for years her mother lived there too—advice: You're lucky, take it, and take care of your man. Sometime she'd sing in the basement like a soprano bird, her voice, a glass of sweet tea on a summer day. He liked to brag. Tell anybody who'd listen about how he didn't love anybody more than he loved himself, paid all the bills, about how she didn't have to do nothin' but take care of him. Left out what a spirit-killing job this was, left out that after cancer that started in her back and spread, she didn't fight it because she was tired of living and ready to go home to her Father. He was already living with his long time woman when Ruth died—had everything that reminded me of her removed the same day. In all those years, I never saw her cry. Used to tell myself I'd never let a man do me like this.

In 1998, I wrote a monologue combining part of her story, my story, and the stories of other Black women I've known and fiction in an attempt to empathize or more intimately identify with her lived experience of long-term abuse and accomplish something I'd always wanted for her—escape:

Woman in the Tree

(*sings*) It's not easy being green! Ooooooooh, I usetalooooooove that man. Tall-wavy-head-cut-ten-speed-bike-ridin'-milk shake drinkin'…beautiful (*pause*) butter wouldn't melt in his mouth but I would. He was my everything. When I was fifteen, I'd watch him playin' ball with his shirt off in the courtyard, body ripplin' and sweatin', ignorin' me, laughin' with his boys…but I didn't care (*pause*) some time I'd wait for him all day, just hopin' he'd glance my way, let me carry his wet towel, run get him somethin' cool to drink—anything, I was pitiful (*pause*) Years went by, I got cuter, he got finer and FINALLY one day he noticed me…that was the beginning. (*pause*) Drinkin' wasn't the problem…Hear me? DRINKIN' WAS 'NOT' the problem! (*pause*) Took me a long time to realize that…a lifetime to be exact. It may have been HIS problem…suckin' up whiskey bottles like he'd suck in his gut when he crawled in at 2, 3, 4, 5 o'clock in the mornin'. His mama thought he was cute…thought the shit he did to me…was cute. (*voice change*) "He don't mean nothin' by it" she'd say with that sugar-sweet-but-really-I-hate-your-ass-bitch high tone voice-a hers. "He was drunk." (*pause*) Worse part is…I believed her. Believed her right through two broken noses, two broken arms, two…body casts. Through it all I didn't have to ask myself, nobody HAD to ask me (although almost everybody I knew did) WHY don't you leave him? I already knew…I loved him! I'd gone to church every Sunday the good Lord brought around and I knew that a woman's place was in the home, in the kitchen, in the bedroom, any place her husband was, and without a doubt that place was until death. (*pause*) I was young and wantin' to be in love when I met him. I was easy. Measured my own value based on the look in a young man's eyes…if he wanted me I was worth somethin'. (*pause*) First ten years were the hardest. I was young, lookin' for either cupid or my knight in shining armor each night like a dummy, what I got was…woke up in the middle of the night, snatched outta bed (*voice change*) "You stankin' ass bitch where you been? Shut up! I called here at EXACT-LY 10:27 p.m. and you didn't answer the phone! What were you doin'? Up here givin' it to somebody in my bed? Huh! You yellow piece of shit! (*pause*) I'd sit very quietly, not even thinkin' of air, holdin' each hair in place on my head, holdin' my heart in its case, holdin' on…waitin' for the moment to pass…or not. (*pause*) Usually he'd start laughin' real loud, sometime holdin' one of his guns to my head clickin', one time firing a round off into the ceiling (Police never came, neighbors never complained)…For days afterward, I'd cook his favorite things for dinner, massage his tired feet, wash his ass…anything to make him forgive me. (*pause*) See I knew I'd done somethin' wrong…just didn't know what it was. 'Cause he LOVED me so he had to have a reason…Didn't he? (*pause*) Sometime he'd come home so drunk he was funny. Steadawantin' to kick my ass, he'd gently kiss me, tellin' me some of the jokes he'd heard in the streets that night, makin' me see that young man in the playground I fell in love with again. (*pause*) He couldn't hold it when he was drunk. And since he was too lazy keep getting' up, he kept a bucket beside the bed and he'd just roll over relieve himself and go back to sleep. (*pause*) I refused to dump that bucket, so quiet-as-it's-kept—it was usually full. This particular night, wasn't in no mood for ha ha…I had one arm in a cast and he hadn't been home in four days…I just wanted him to lay his ass down, go to sleep and leave me alone, but Noooooo! Here he come…Well he made a mistake, kicked that bucketa pee and wet up his new Stacy Adams. (*pause*) Before I could stop myself, I started to laugh…deep down in my toes, out the tips of my fingers, even my forehead was laughin'. (*pause*) Know what that bastard did? He dumped the resta that bucket on my head and stood there, holdin' his hand over my mouth while it dripped down. I started to turn green…first my feet turned green, the skin on them smooth and new as a baby's ass…I looked at my hands, they turned green and the scars from where he used to bite me disappeared…then in a single, warm, loving move, the rest of me turned green.

Dreamgirl was the iris of her father's eye; her mother's deferred dream and a loving brother's only sister. She was lovely inside and out, smart, community minded and down to earth. Our family just knew she was going to be one of us who made it to a better life. She moved to New York to attend law school—returned with an Associate degree and started dating this young man we could tell was a fool the first time she brought him to a family reunion. He wouldn't leave her side, wouldn't make eye contact with any of us and sat the entire time either staring at her or off into space.

What happened to her is filtered through secondhand mouths. I don't re-member who told me what happened that night, but they got the story from the person who found her and her baby son. We'd been hearing for weeks that they were arguing all the time, but tried not to worry too much because we knew her father lived only a short distance away. Early in the evening *Dreamgirl* told her man she was going to leave him. Her man didn't stop her. He waited until right after she'd strapped their son in the car seat and got into her SUV. Before she could start the truck, he approached the driver's side, shot once through the window striking her in the head. He left their son in the car—returned to their apartment and shot himself. Both dead at the scene. Their only son left in the back seat. She was days away from her 25th birthday.

This morning I woke up. *Triste*'s obituary greeted me on top of the 4-drawer file cabinet where it's stood for the last 4 years. Her image on the front of it was beautiful, vibrant, and in living color like she was. One more time I weep. I listen to Donny Hathaway, who jumped out of a window believing no one in the world loved him, and I weep for *Triste*. I've been waiting for her to help me write about this ache her death has left in my family's heart. I think of my daughter *Marla*, one of the last to see her alive, who told *Triste* repeatedly *that mothafucka's crazy*, who tried to get *Triste* to run away, to stay at her house, until she could get herself together. When my daughter rewinds that moment in our conversations, she always pauses as time never does to remember, to wish she woulda, to ask if there's anything else she could have done or said that day to convince our cousin to come with her—She repeats what *Triste*'s man, the father of the unborn child she carried said when he saw my daughter in the shopping mall that day: *You don't like me very much do you?*

It's the day of *Triste*'s funeral. We, a large family of 5 generations that started with 8 girls and 3 boys in the late 1800s pack the huge church, all kinds of folks from every corner of *Triste*'s short life have come to pay their respects, to comfort, to cry like Grief has one shoulder. There are flowers all around her snow-white coffin, her brother *Ike*, destined to die less than two years later, stands by the coffin, his eyes shades, his stance that of a Marine on guard duty. On the big-time screen are images of *Triste*, her daughter and son, her dreams for becoming a doctor. The pastor tries to bring joy into the space, to get Christian folks to shout, to praise the name of God, to be grateful *Triste*'s with him. and I want to jump up and shout *Bullshit, ain't one mothafuckin' thing to be happy about except the mothafucka that killed her, killed himself, she DEAD ya'll, DEAD at 22 years old and there ain't nothin' we can do but mourn.*

People kept getting up to speak and when the pastor tried to move on *Ike* stepped up like a warrior fighting and stopped his hand. *Ike* said: *We gon' take our time, 'cause I ain't never gon' see my sister again.* And people kept coming. Sorrow set up house in me and wouldn't leave, my dress soggy with death, my mind shifting to my daughter sitting beside me beside herself, in the end stepping up to say something loving about her cuz. I felt mama sitting on my other side hold her breath afraid of what my daughter would say. I was proud, and ashamed to be grateful it wasn't her lying there sunglasses hiding eyes that had to be removed.

I never saw *Ike's* eyes. Too proud to let the world see how he saw himself believing he'd let his sister down, not understanding that he didn't. A woman begins to sing *His Eye Is on the Sparrow* and I think of those small, small birds and how safe they are in the air, in the trees they live in, in bird world where domestic violence and murder of bird mamas does not exist. I wish to God my cousin could have shape shifted that day—changed as suddenly as calm comes after storms into a beautiful sparrow, escaped the last sound she heard, lived to take her babies home. And for a moment she's spared, I see her lifted up on a July summer breeze, ancestor spirits in the air to guide her. But the song is just a song. It reminds of God's love, but can't spare anything and as the sistah finishes one more chorus, I feel myself get up, tell my daughter I can't stay, catch mama's eyes as she reaches for her purse. We exit quickly having paid our respects, angry at something that happened with no one to punish, blaming everything. My daughter stayed to the end, reporting how *Ike* tried to stop them from closing the coffin, how he screamed and hollered at the graveyard trying to stop them from lowering her body into the ground. My daughter shared how he cried like he wanted to die right then, how he thought everybody was mad at him—but her.

Four years later I write looking out of my office window that looks out on the fork in a road, a world suddenly crying after days and days of no rain I think of all the unknown, young Black women like *Triste*, of how long it took the police to come that day when her aunt called the police screaming for help. Of how by the time they got there, her man had broken through her aunt's door, ran upstairs where she was hiding, put the gun to her head and when she said *I don't wanta die,* shot killing her and their unborn baby, of how he then turned the gun on himself.

Bop: Stop![2]
Black women are murdered every day in my hometown,
everywhere it feels like I'm getting black eyes, scars, my neck
wrung like a chicken, I hear their voices, see their skin, eyes,
noses, mouths, hairlines when I look in the mirror
to put lipstick on a mouth stuck in permanent O of shock, sadness
words I speak to sistas all over the country double checking door locks.

Stop in the name of love, before you break my heart.
In the midst of this Valentine's Day comes and goes, the flowers
and card my husband gives me like every year, disappear in a puff of smoke
when my mind can't stop pining about what's wrong, about the unidentified
dead mamas waiting in the county morgue, toe tags missing names
breasts frozen in moment they lost everything. Most days I try to leave
my heart at home safe in bed I share with man who loves me like
ain't no tomorrow, but when I get into my car I find it on the seat,

leaping to bring hard rage I feel like a storm.

Stop in the name of love, before you break my heart.

Every Friday right after eagle lands me and my circle of sistas
gather like stars in same universe, share things we tell ourselves
to make us feel safe, our almost-happened stories that always end in tears
we shed and re-gather like sweat pouring down one face. We laugh
at small things that are only funny because we want to seem
like we have it all together, like we're not afraid of the dark.

Stop in the name of love, before you break my heart.
Mary E. Weems

Motherwit

1. A man who loves you will not abuse you.
2. Once a man's abused you, he will do it again unless he gets the kind of help you cannot give him.
3. He's not really sorry.
4. You cannot change him.
5. You can change yourself.
6. Getting help starts with acknowledgment of the abuse.
7. Reach out for support from family, friends, and/or professionals.
8. Do not listen to women who encourage you to stay and work it out.
9. Do not tell him you're leaving. Leave, then at your leisure, let him know you're not coming back.
10. Don't go back.
11. Learn to love yourself and you won't allow this to happen again—ever.
12. Filing a legal Protection or Restraining Order will not help unless he decides to stay away from you.
13. If a man hurts you physically: (1) Get away from him a.s.a.p. (2) Have someone take pictures of your injuries (3) Go to the emergency room for care and make certain the visit is recorded (4) File charges with your local Prosecutor's Office.

Outside Resources

A quick online search will provide a number of resources for women seeking help.
Here I share a few of them:

- There are Safe Houses located in many communities. These spaces are kept hidden for obvious reasons, but their locations will be made available through any local or national organization involved in providing assistance to women in trouble.

- National Domestic Violence Hotline. http://www.thehotline.org/ Caution: Use a safe computer [Note: No computer is completely safe] or call 1-800-799-SAFE(7233) or TTY 1-800-787-3224. Date Accessed: 6-25-11.
- HelpGuide.org. http://www.helpguide.org. Goal of this organization is: "[T]o empower you with the knowledge and support you need to take charge of your life." Site provides free online resources that are "motivating, balanced and free." Date Accessed: 6-25-11.

Notes

1. Pseudonyms have been used to protect the identity of family members. I use a backslash between auto and ethnography because when I write based upon my lived experience as a Black woman, I'm always including the lived experiences of other Black women because there is an inextricable racial, gender, and cultural connection between us that both consciously and unconsciously enters my words as I write from a collective and spiritual, rather than an individual, mindset.
2. Black poet Afaa M. Weaver created the Bop poetic form during a Cave Canem retreat. Not unlike the Shakespearean sonnet, the Bop is a poetic argument consisting of three stanzas, each stanza followed by a repeated line, or refrain, and each undertaking a different purpose in the overall argument of the poem. First stanza (six lines) states the problem, the second (eight lines) expands upon the problem, the third stanza (six lines) either resolves the problem or documents the failure to solve it.

References

Lorde, A. (1984). *Sister outsider: Essays and speeches*. Berkeley, CA: The Crossing Press.
Richardson, L. (1994). Writing a method of inquiry. In N. Denzin & L. Richardson (Eds.), *Handbook of qualitative research* (pp. 516–529). Thousand Oaks, CA: Sage.

eight

A Telephone Call

Norman K. Denzin

I was caught in a series of dreams, painful memories about mother, father, my grandfather. I'd dozed off on the morning train to Chicago listening to Bob Dylan's song "Series of Dreams" (1991). Like in his dream, "everything was coming to the top, nothing was staying down where it's wounded. Nothing was coming to a permanent stop" [This is what I copied from the Internet: I was thinking of a series of dreams, Where nothing comes up to the top. Everything stays down where it's wounded, And comes to a permanent stop.] I woke up screaming inside my head.

I agree with William Kittridge (1994): we have to be careful about the stories we tell about ourselves. We have to be careful about our dreams too. We might get caught inside a story or a series of dreams we don't want to be in.

This is what happened to mother and me. We were on the telephone together. It was right after Mother's Day, 1996. We were getting along pretty good. I was following up on a call I'd made a week earlier. I'd called to say we couldn't come for dinner that weekend because my father was going into the hospital for an operation and I felt I should be there. She didn't let on that this was a problem, so we missed dinner and I was there when my father came out of surgery. I thought everything was going O.K. between the two of us.

Mother and I got into talking and telling stories that neither one of us could accept. I think I told her a story about myself that she didn't like. She told me a story about my father that I didn't like. In fact she said I was just like my father.

We got into quite a battle over this. It was all happening on the telephone. Somehow all communication fell apart after that. I think we stopped trusting one another. Anyway, I mark this conversation as one of the last we ever had. Of course she's still alive, so we might talk again, sometime, but I doubt if that will happen. Not from my end it won't.

The telephone call really started with a letter. Back in May of 1981 I was in Minneapolis in a treatment center, getting help for my drinking problem. I was assigned to a psychiatrist, a young fellow, Dr. James. We got along pretty well. He had me take the MMPI, which I really got into.

The results came back and we sat down together. I was on the edge of my bed, he was on a chair in front of me. Out the window I could see geese flying south. It was still cold, for the month of May.

He started out, "Was there a strong father figure in your life? Someone who hurt you?"

I said, "Yes, and No, My father left when I was 18, and he was never really home when I was growing up."

"Humm." He made a little humming noise. "Think again. It looks like you have a lot of anger toward somebody in your family."

"Mostly my mother, she was sick a lot. She kind of used being sick as a way to get her own way."

"Sounds passive aggressive to me. Did your mother like men?"

"I think she hated my father at the end."

"How about her father?"

"They always fought, but he gave her everything she ever asked for."

"Your mother is a passive-aggressive woman. She used her illness to control men. Your mother has been controlling you. Did you know that?"

"Well, I have a lot of anger. She has not spoken to me since 1973. I feel kind of abandoned. I never understood how she could not love my daughters, her granddaughters. But she just cut them out of her life."

"Your mother is a very sick woman. She uses anger and passivity to control people."

This all started to make sense. Then the psychiatrist switched topics.

"On the MMPI you score high on somatic illness factors. Do you suffer from some physical pain, or illness?"

"Yes. My back. I have chronic back pain. It gets worse when I'm under a lot of stress. Lately it has been killing me, but who wants to be here?"

"I think your back pain is connected to your mother. When you feel stress, check and see if your back starts to act up. This pain is your body telling you that you are under stress. I think you should write your mother. Do you have her address? Tell her you forgive her for what she did to you, and ask her to forgive you for what you did to her."

Well that minute the back pain started to leave, and it has only come back once since, that day she told me the story about my father. Well, it really wasn't a story, she just compared me to him.

I wrote that letter. It went to Cottonwood, Arizona, and came back, addressee unknown. I sent it back, and it came back again. My father told me to send it five times. The fifth time it came back in the form of a phone call. My mother was on the other end of the line. "Hi, this is Mother. How are you?"

One thing led to another, and 7 months later, after not seeing her for 23 years, she was living two miles away, not even across town.

We settled into a routine. I'd see her and George, my stepfather, about once a week. At that time my wife was driving 180 miles a day to a job clear across the state. I was not real happy about this, but mother and I were getting along pretty well, and I think she enjoyed the fact that she was home, when my wife was gone.

As I said, I was on the phone to mother, touching base after the last phone call when I'd said I was going over to Iowa to be with Dad when he had his operation. That's when she started in, kind of out of the blue.

"Did you go to a psychiatrist when you were in the hospital? If you were a real man, you wouldn't have needed to go to a psychiatrist."

"Mother, he helped me. He helped get me going to A.A. " She would have none of this.

"You're weak, just like your father. He went to those A.A. meetings too. If he had been half a man he wouldn't have needed them."

I couldn't let this stand. "Mother, I resent that. A.A. helped him."

She wouldn't allow this. "You know he left with that woman he met in A.A. What was her name? I suppose you thought that was O.K."

I was not going to touch that with a 10-foot pole. "Mother, lets don't get into that. He did what he had to do. I've forgiven him."

"Well, I haven't."

"That's your business."

"So why did you go to that psychiatrist anyway?"

"Mother!" I was yelling by this time. "He helped me!"

"Well, I don't need that kind of help, and you shouldn't have gone to see him."

Now she was screaming. In the background I could hear George telling her to calm down. On my end, Kathy, my wife, was doing the same. I tried to crank it down a little bit.

"Mother, let's not fight. I told you this about Dad because we agreed to have an honest, open relationship. No secrets. Now I think I shouldn't have told you." This appeased her a little and she apologized for yelling. "I'm sorry."

I wanted out, so I said, "Kathy would like to say Hi." Kathy got on the line and invited her to lunch.

They went to lunch, and the next time I saw her, mother said, "Boy she sure drives fast in that little car of hers. It's real cute. How do you feel about her working? You know I don't think women should work, what do you think? Don't you think Nathan [my stepson] needs his mother at home?"

I didn't want to get into a big fight, but I said, "I think women should work if they want to. But it's none of my business." Mother demurred. "My, that's interesting. "This is the last time we talked.

* * *

Actually I lie. We talked two more times. She and George came for Christmas dinner but barely spoke to any of us. They were real quiet, kind of withdrawn. They left right after dessert.

"Thank you for a lovely dinner." She stood on the lower step of the front porch. She was wearing one of her Western outfits, fancy cowboy boots, silver belt, big buckle, turquoise necklace, red bandanna, Elizabeth Taylor bangs, red lipstick. She looked back over her shoulder as George led her to the car.

She called when they got home. "Thank you for a lovely dinner," and hung up. She never called again. We never spoke again.

* * *

In my series of dreams on the train to Chicago, Mother was talking to me again. She was talking to my grandfather, and to my father. I was on the sidelines, watching. Part of me was stuck inside our fight over dad and that psychiatrist. It was all mixed up.

"Daddy, you never told me you were my real father. You lied and told Momma that you got me from a poor family in Muscatine. Why didn't you tell the truth? Why did you leave us in that fancy hotel in Kansas City and go off with that other woman? Momma never forgave you."

"Kenneth, how could you leave with that woman from A.A.? You are just like Daddy, and now Norman is just like you!"

* * *

An Iowa farmhouse. Late spring. I'm sitting at the top of the stairs, outside Grandma's bedroom. She's dead now. I'd found a letter in her safe. I was drunk. The letter was dated October 30, 1919. It was to grandma and grandpa. It was from a woman with a Muscatine, Iowa, address. "Please take good care of my baby girl. Elizabeth Katherine. God bless you."

* * *

At this point in my dreams there was no exit. All four of us were trapped in the same room, and Mother has having her fury out on all of us. I had that letter in my hand. There was no place to run. I had witnessed a crime, a series of crimes against Mother. We were all trying to run away. In a flash I understood her anger at me that day on the telephone. Elizabeth (nee Betty) Katherine Townsley Denzin Campbell, formal first name Elizabeth, had dreamed a life for herself. She even looked like a famous Elizabeth. Her anger, buried for a lifetime, burned like a long-simmering fire. She had never been properly loved. Her response was to punish, punish herself, punish those she might have one day loved.

In her dreams, a series of dreams, she was always wounded, surrounded by weak, unfaithful men who needed to be controlled, controlled through guilt, illness, guile, a Liz Taylor smile, winks, a toss of the head, cowboy boots, tight-fitting blue jeans, and silver belts. Hello, this is your Mother.

* * *

He died on November 15, 2005, 13 months before she did. They were living 30 miles apart, he in Amana, Iowa, she in Lone Tree, six miles from Grandpa's farm. Near Rock Island, standing on the top deck of the Delta Queen, I threw his ashes on the waters of the Mississippi River. The wind blew them back, his ashes stuck to my arms. Mother was cremated, too. The caller from the nursing home was terse. "Your mother died yesterday. She was cremated yesterday. She gave me explicit instructions. I was not to call you until after she had been cremated."

* * *

It started and ended with a telephone call.

References

Dylan, B. (1991). Series of dreams. Special Rider Music. Colombia Records.
Kittridge, W. (1994). *Hole in the sky.* San Francisco, CA: Murray House.

◟nine◞

Tell It
A Contemporary Chorale for Black Youth Voices

Durell Callier

On September 29, 2009, I received word that one of my students, Tyrone Williams, had been brutally slain while visiting his Chicago home for the weekend.[1] The news stung the back of my throat like gall, and as tears cascaded down my face I wondered why and how? Tyrone was a bright, inquisitive student with a great sense of humor and an impeccable work ethic—a full-time student maintaining two jobs with a solid GPA. Like me, Tyrone was a first-generation, young, Black male from a working-class background. In the days following Tyrone's death I found myself consoling students, mourning with co-workers and peers who mentored and/or knew Tyrone. As life careened ahead, I needed to remember the moments of life Tyrone and I shared together—so I wrote. I wrote for the countless Tyrones whose bodies lie wasted in our bustling cities, whose names don't make the 6 o'clock news, whose gravestones read "Gone too soon." I wrote to remember, for revolution, to heal and be vulnerable again. The result was "Take Back Life I," a poem in remembrance of Tyrone Williams, Percy Day, and Derrion Albert.[2]

Tell It: A Contemporary Chorale for Black Youth Voices began at the rupture, which was Tyrone. It is an homage to AudreLorde's (1990) Need: A Chorale for Black Woman Voices. Lorde's chorale ends with a quote by Barbara Deming:[3] "We can not live without our lives." Where Need ends, so I begin. Tell It tells—of joy, sorrow, violence, the lives and deaths of Black youth in particular and urban youth in general. In its declaration and therefore affirmation of the sacredness and value of life, Tell It acts as a witness,[4] demanding us all to bear responsibility as witnesses to the stories and lives of urban youth.I now present to you Tell It: A Contemporary Chorale for Black Youth Voices.

Movement I: Day Breaks / Heart Aches[5]

Setting takes place at the intersection of Anywhere USA and The Forgotten Avenue, which should be urban in display. Begin scene with pedestrian traffic, where various stage crossings occur. There should be a group of teenagers standing on the corner, huddled, with some leaning on the wall. <Cue music: Moment 4 Life[6]><Lights fade up> Scene opens with sounds reminiscent of a neighborhood summer scene. Upstage center girls are jumping rope, with downstage left (V7) singing "Tell It." Sitting on one of the stoops reading a newspaper and surveying the neighborhood is V1.

V7: (female lead throughout) Tell it

All Voices: Tell it/ Tell it like it is uh-oh

V7: Tell it

All Voices: Tell it/ Tell it like it is uh-oh

V7: My name is (insert name)

All Voices: Tell it tell it

V7: I'm on the line

All Voices: Tell it tell it

V7: And I can do it

All Voices: Tell it tell it

V7: With a (insert Zodiac sign)

All Voices: Tell it tell it

V7: And you know whut

All Voices: Whutttt

V7: And you know whut

All Voices: Whutttt

V7: My man was rollin on the ocean, he was rollin on the sea but the best thing about it he was rollin on me

All Voices: (trailing off) Tell it, Tell it/ Tell it like it is uh-oh

Chorus members fade into background. Lines below performed in canon with slow deliberate speed, whereas each line builds and is connected to the one preceding and following it.

V1: (slow as if gasping for air) I have been try-ing to honor life

V1: But DEATH you have been making this very

All Voices: (in round robin form, various deliveries) oh so very

V1: hard/ In light of recent events....The shooting and death of one of my students

V2: Tyrone Williams, 19

V1: His cousin

V2: Percy Day, 17

V1: The beating and death of

V2: Derrion Albert, 16

V1: The decapitation, dismemberment and partial burning of

V3: Jorge Steven Lopez Mercado,[7] 19

V1: The state sanctioned, court ruled "accidental" death of

V4: Kiwane Carrington,[8] 15

V1:The stabbing murder—death of

V5: Sakia Gunn, 15

V1: And countless others who I know not of,

V6: (with care) Tanja Stokes,[9] 8

V1: whose names evade our memory

V6: (with care) Ariana Jones, 7

V7 (interchangeably female/male): The Atlanta Child Murders[10]: Edward Hope Smith, 14; Alfred James Evans, 13; Milton Harvey, 14; Yusef Ali Bell, 9; Angel Lanier, 12; Jeffrey L. Mathis, 10; Eric Middlebrooks, 14; Christopher P. Richardson, 11; Latonya Wilson, 7; Aaron D. Wyche, 10; Anthony Bernard Carter, 9; Earl Lee Terrell, 10; Clifford Jones, 13

V1: And whose deaths all seem

V1, V2, V4: (slow and deliberate) so very justified

V1, V5, V6: (slow and deliberate) so very necessary

V7: as if just the status quo

(V8 enters, s/he should be wearing distinctively different clothing from the rest of the setting, equipped with a small, ruffled notepad, voice recording device, and pen)

V1: (pause) But instead I have decided to take this moment to honor not death

But living

V8: (to V1) Sir may I have a moment of your time

(Absent chorus members filter back on stage)

Chorus

V7: (V7 male lead for chorus) Tell it

All Voices: Tell it/ Tell it like it is uh-oh

V2: Tell it

All Voices: Tell it/ Tell it like it is uh-oh

V2: My name is Ty

All Voices: Tell it tell it

V2: I'm on the line

All Voices: Tell it, tell it

(Chorus fades down, as conversation between V8 and V1 takes precedence)

Movement II: Good Kids

V8: Could you tell me about Tyrone Williams, are you familiar with his story

V1: "Williams was home for the weekend from the University of Illinois in Urbana-Champaign, where he was a student, to get an outfit to wear to a home-coming dance at the school."[11]

(Lights fade down and should be dimly lit, with spotlights on V1, V2, V7 (female) and V8. A re-enactment of the night should occur as V8 recants events from the night)

V8: Saturday, September 26, 2009—family members were at a loss Saturday about why two cousins were fatally shot outside one of the teen's home in the Homan Square neighborhood. Sharnia Goodman was having a laugh with cousins Percy Day, 17, and Tyrone Williams, 19, outside the two-flat in the 3700 block of West Polk Street when she said somebody opened fire at about 9:15 p.m.

V7: "We saw him walking up the block, then he stopped a few houses down, turned and walked away"

V8: said Goodman, who was Day's girlfriend.

V7: "About 10 minutes later he came back, the shooting started and everybody tried to run."

V8: The shooter was not familiar to any of them, and they had no interaction with the man before he opened fire, Goodman said.

(Lights fade up. V1 and V8 resume conversation. Neighborhood interactions continue)

V1: "They were good kids. Good kids. They rarely ventured past the front steps when they were out here, and we have never had any kind of trouble on this block. It's all turned around. This just doesn't make any sense."

(V8 moves to group of youth standing at the corner, V7 (male voice 1) begins lines)

Movement III: Autophobia[12]

V7 (male voice 1, to V8): Are you afraid of the dark?/I used to be/That dim quiet smoothness/Vulnerable coolness/Midnight skin/Bumps in the night/Terrors of the imagination/Hooded strangers/Thieves coming to rob you/Rape your women/Always male/About my height or taller/My complexion or darker/Baggy jeans, and a white tee/Media induced frenzies of

V2: Me

V7(male voice 1): Bombarding your motherboards/Cascading across TV screens

V3: Me

V7 (male voice 1): Downloaded onto desktops

V4: Me

V7 (male voice 1): Distributed on handouts

V6: Me

V7 (male voice 2): Drudged up from the annals of history

V6: Me

V7 (male voice 1): Mongrel, infidel, coon,

V7 (female voice 3): Me

V7 (male voice 1): Mammy, pappy, nigger

V2: Me

V7 (male voice 1): Wetback, chink, kike

V3: Me

V7 (male voice 1): Faggot, sissy, carpet muncher

V5: Me

V7 (male voice 1): I used to be afraid of the dark

V1: Until I learned, it was me

V7 (female voice 2): Until I learned

V7 (male 1 and female voice: 2,3) Til I came to know

V7 (female voice 1,3): Realized

V7 (male voice 2, female voice 2): That it was

V7 (male voice 1, 3): Is

V7 (female voice 1): Simply

V7 (male voice 1): Me

V8 (as if searching for words, or creating a headline): Bumps in the night/Terrors of the imagination/Hooded strangers/Media induced frenzies of

V6: Me

V7 (male voice 1): Of YOU <pause> Now are you still afraid of the dark?

Movement IV: Street Lights

(Lights dim, as V5 moves downstage on The Forgotten Avenue, wearing baggy jeans, a loose fitting shirt and durag, she is not discernibly female to an "untrained eye")

V5: "I learned to sag my jeans just right by watching the men around me. Studied the way they rocked tilted fitted caps over crisp tapers and deep waves. Matchin kicks, neatly creased jeans 'throwback' jerseys, that was my style,"[13] our style, girls who dressed like boys, often mistaken for teenage boys because. We have the courage to dress the way we feel inside. We are your daughters, sisters and nieces. We are young, black, lesbians. Our courage makes you uncomfortable. Our authenticity scares you.(pause)

(Spotlight on V5's face)
V5: Me and my crew Newark, New Jersey. After a night out, we had just got off the bus. Then this car pulls up. We already knew what they wanted.

(Chorus members in arc surround V5, solo females first, then males join similarly)

No

V7 (male voice): Hey girl
V7 (male voice): I'm just tryin to holla

No

V7 (female voice): He got out the car

No

V7 (female voice): Richard Mc-Cullough

We're gay
No

V7 (male voice): you know you want it
V7 (male voice): Slut
V7 (female voice): No

No

V7 (male voice): Dyke
V7 (male voice): Bitch

No

V7 (female voice): Movin closer
V7 (female voice): A knife

No

V7 (female voice): Safety

Fighting for my life

V7 (female voice): No means no
V7 (male voice): No

Stabbed

V7 (female voice): A knife

Bled out

V7 (female voice): Fighting for our lives

Board and Market

Mothers Day Morning

V7 (male voice): No

Bled out

<V5 exits stage into audience>
<All cast members enter stage, with
candles, creating a memorial at the
corner of Anywhere USA and The
Forgotten Avenue. Consider non-
traditional items, what should be
memorialized should be of importance
not only to cast but to youth—items
which resonate familial/family remem-
brances.>
V7 (male voice): Mama don't cry[14]

There wasn't nothin you did wrong
This life choice as you so call it
Was if we believe choosing is in-
volved…mine

Mama don't cry
You didn't raise no Twinkie for a man
You weren't ill equipped
Nor robbed me of anything cause cir-
cumstances required that only women's
hands would steer this one

Mama don't you cry
I've cried sea fulls enough for the both
of us
Drowned myself in them
Been baptized anew
Washed over, and healed
And you know it was you who taught
me the power of a tear
The necessity of release

V7 (female voice): No

V7 (female voice): No

V7 (female voice): Sakia
V7 (female voice): No
V7 (female voice): Sakia
V7 (female voice): No
V7 (female voice): Sakiaaaa
<Chorus members separate. As Chorus
members separate V3 enters with rose >
V3: Jorge Steven Lopez Mercado

V3: Mama don't cry

V8: A very well known person in the
gay community of Puerto Rico, and
very loved. Jorge was found on the
site of an isolated road in the city of
Cayey.[15]
V3: Mama don't you cry

Mama don't cry

The sanctity, cleansing, life giving,
anger freeingness of it all
The vulnerable strength it required

Mama don't cry	V8: He was partially burned,
I am strong	decapitated, and dismembered, both
I am healthy	arms, both legs, and the torso.
I am intelligent	
I am survivin on my own	
I got street smarts	
I still love God	V3: Don't cry
And knows without a shadow of a	
doubt that God loves even me	
Mama don't cry	
I will make it	
I am loving me ALL of me now a days	Don't cry
Mama please…	
Please don't you cry	
You ain't failed nobody	
This could not have been prevented	
This was oh so necessary	V8: Never in the history of Puerto Rico
It was pre-destined before either of us	has a murder been classified as a hate
came to know the other	crime.
	V3: Don't cry remember your
	words,"Love conquers hate"[16]
Mama don't cry	
I am gay	
And that doesn't change a bit of who	
I was	V3: Don't cry
Who I am,	
Nor who I will become	
If you must cry	
Cry over the accomplishments	V3: Remember
Rejoice in tears that I weep no more	
If you must cry	
Cry about the love that we share	
Let each tear careen down your cheek	
	V3: Remember
If you gonna cry	Love, conquers hate
Cry knowing	Remember

That you did   V3: Love, conquers hate
ABSOLUTELY NOTHING   Remember
WRONG BUT LOVE
ME AS ME....And that, that Mama—   Love Conquers Hate
AIN'T NEVA WRONG!   Love
<V3 exits downstage before leaving,   Conquers Hate
offers rose to audience, placing it on
stage edge>   V3: Love...conquers...hate

Movement V: Moment 4 Life

V7 (female voice): I want you to know and remember my cousin, Brandi Rose Hobson (September 20,1983–September 2, 2001). Raped and strangled 9 yrs ago in Chicago. She was my beautiful, open, and fun cousin. I hold sweet Alabama and Chicago summertime memories of her.[17](places memorial object on corner after delivery of lines)

V1: You See I am TRY-ING to take back life/ These tears are not of sadness/ No, no defeat lies here/Today I must remember/ Have you remember/That life is about living/That we weep in our coming in/ But rejoice in our going out/ Today I refuse/ ABSOLUTELY, refuse to allow death to have yet another victory/ So what these atrocities happened in cities distant from here/ Hell in your own back yard Chicago, Puerto Rico, Champaign-Urbana, Atlanta, Baltimore, Detroit, Oakland, Saint Louis, Compton.

(Crowd dissipates, blowing out candles as they exit stage. V1 and V8 are left on stage. V8 rapidly takes notes of what V1 says. Lights gradually fade up and feel sharp like a burst of light in contrast to the previous darkness of the scene)

V1: So what they were black, brown, gay/ Male/ Female/ So what they were young/ So what, so what!?/ This could have been anywhere/ Any city/ So what, so what? This is everywhere/ This is most cities/ These are not exceptions/ No, these are common day casualties/ Casualties of some war we are desperately losing/ Some war we deny is at our very own doorsteps/ In our very own homes/ Beaming in from our televisions/ Streaming across the internet/ Downloading right onto our desktops/ There is nothing to fear/ But this threat is real/ Very real/ These deaths real/ Very real/ And I refuse/ I refuse any longer to sob/ Refuse any longer to cry/ Refuse any longer to pain/ Over death/ No today/ Today I remind you/ Remind me, that life is about living/ So do it!/ Do it freely/

(All other cast members begin to filter back on stage assuming previous positions from Movement I)

V1: Do it justly/ Do it as if it is the last thing you could ever do/ Because it/ JUST/ MIGHT/ BE!/ But (my God) do it/ Love it/ Cherish it/ Make it Sacred/ Remember it/ Remember to live/ For I today/ Challenge us/ That we not mourn, and give death yet another victory/ But that we live/ Live life/ Life live/ Live!/ Live Life fearlessly/ Take back our streets!/ Take back the day!/ Take back even the night/ But (my God) Take back life!

Movement VI: Just Another Day

V7: (female lead changing lead throughout)

V7: Tell it

All Voices: Tell it/ Tell it like it is uh-oh

V2: Tell it

All Voices: Tell it/Tell it like it is uh-oh

Continues as background chant while Voices fade in and out delivering lines

(Lines below performed in canon with slow deliberate speed, whereas each line builds, and is connected to the one preceding and following it)

V1: These stories needed tellin
V2: Tellincuz

V7 (male voice):Cuz we were human
V5: Were real

V1: Cuz they needed ta be told
V6: Are human
V3:So they might be of use to some-
one
V2: Cuz if I hold it in then it's only
mine

V4: Because if I hold it in then it's only
mine

V3: Dies with me
V6: Cuz if I hold it in then nobody
else will know

V2: Cuz if I hold it in then it's only
mine
V1: Cuz if I hold on to them

V1:Tyrone Williams

V2: Percy Day

V1: Derrion Albert

V3: Jorge Steven Lopez Mercado

V4: Kiwane Carrington

V1: Sakia Gunn <pause> if I hold em
in, then nobody else will know

V6: Tanja Stokes

V1: And countless others, names I may never know, Atlanta child murders, Amber alerts never found, Amber alerts never sounded cuz

V6: Too poor

V2: Gay

V6: Too much not what u needed

V6: time of day

V4: Ran across the wrong authority
V7 (round robin): If we keep silent

V1: Ariana Jones

V7: <Chorus of Tell It increases>

V5: Cause the child was too Black

V1: Too queer

V5: Butch

V2: Too much in da wrong place, wrong time, wrong city, block, hood, time of night

V1: Refuse of the state were they

V1: nobody else will know

Chorus:(Decrescendo)

V7: Tell it

All Voices: Tell it/ Tell it like it is uh-oh

V7: Tell it

All Voices: Tell it/ Tell it like it is uh oh (retard this line)

(Silence) (Lights Down)

Barrage of sounds building upon one another in no particular order. Layered entrances, with childlike fun beginning, interrupted by city sounds, ending in a gunshot: child-like laughter, double-dutch ropes turning, basketball bouncing, licks of a hand game (e.g., Miss Mary Mack), running, bicycle bell, ice-cream truck, city noises (e.g., horn honking, backing up of trash truck, industrial noises, etc.)

<Gun Sounds><Lights up on V1 as he finishes drawing an outline of a child on the ground. Once finished, he places a kiss with his hand on the forehead of the figure, then places the piece of chalk in the drawn hand, and leaves.><Silence><Cue Music: Moment 4 Life>

Notes

1. See Byrne (2009).
2. See Hawkins (2009).
3. See Deming (1974).
4. To be a witness entails acknowledging one's past—those individuals and communities of ascription/affinity who've influenced you—as well as one's present. Being a witness places one not only as a historian and critic, but as cultural worker—midwife to the dreams and hopes of a people (see Baldwin in Standley& Pratt, 1989). To witness is to remember, to heal and be healed (Alexander, 2005; Bambara, 1980).
5. Notes on the overall structure of Tell It:

    Within Tell It, movements akin to acts are the organizing unit serving as the structure of the play (Castagno, 2001). Unlike acts, which traditionally organize time and events in linear chronology so as to signal a building upon, movements signal a continuum. Rhythm and syncopation, also important, are intended to allow for the overlapping of voices at times and/or the sharing of an idea by multiple voices through the continuation and finishing of that line/ idea. Where words overlap, they are meant to be spoken at the same time. However, there are also times where the script and delivery is delivered in a more traditional dialogue.

    Departing from traditional theatrical usages of characters with particular names, physical attributes, demeanors, and dispositions, I am more interested in the voices of characters and the stories imbued within a voice tonation, rhythm, and juxtaposition with other voices. Therefore, I do not utilize characters but rather (embodied) voices to denote the performers within my piece. The "character" information is as follows:

    Voice 1—narrator, weaving thread throughout piece, male or female voice

    Voice 2—male voice, representative of the stories of Tyrone Williams, Percy Day, and Derrion Albert

    Voice 3—male voice, representative of the story of Jorge Steven Lopez Mercado

    Voice 4—male voice, representative of the story of Kiwane Carrington

    Voice 5— female voice, representative of the story of Sakia Gunn

    Voice 6—female voices, meant to be representative of the stories of 8-year-old Tanja Stokes and her 7-year-old cousin, Ariana Jones

    Voice 7—chorus of voices, interchangeable and at times simultaneously male (3) and female (3), representative of the stories of countless/nameless murdered youth

    Voice 8—"Journalist," representative of media investigation, and coverage
6. See Gumbs (2011).
7. Including Jorge Steven Lopez Mercado, a queer Puerto Rican youth slain in the U.S. Territory of Puerto Rico, underscores the vulnerability created by the relationships of race, sexuality, and age. Gilmore (2007) defines racism as "the state-sanctioned and/or extra-legal production and exploitation of group-differentiated vulnerabilities to premature death, in distinct yet densely interconnected political geographies" (p. 247). Utilizing her definition as a foundation, we must then take into consideration—as the deaths of Jorge and Sakia Gunn highlight—such issues as sexism, classism, homophobia, and so forth, in order to increase the life chances and life opportunities of people of color.
8. See Dolinar (2009).
9. See Coleman (2010).
10. The names, lives, stories and histories of people of color are oftentimes not told, remembered, given substantive media coverage, or allowed critical mass, inquiry, and generative space within our social institutions. Resulting in cultural amnesia, this denigration and denial of memory blocks our access to healing the wounds created by the tragedies and loss suffered by people of color (Alexander, 2005). Remembering, therefore, becomes an antidote to mediate this healing. My attention to listing the names and ages is to help precipitate healing. For Atlanta Child Murders see Baldwin (1985).
11. See Byrne (2009).

12. Autophobia literally means the fear of (phobia) self (auto). Movement III is meant to ask audience members as well as the performers to reflexively analyze their fears. Furthermore, Movement III moves the audience/text beyond a structural critique to understanding the ways in which our individual agency is not only structurally shaped, but how as "free" agents we collude and therefore perpetuate structures of dominance.
13. See Freeman (2008).
14. "Mama Don't Cry (A Queer Son's Tribute to His Mourning Mother)," a poem underscores not only my ethics—personal vulnerability and commitment to justice—but also makes visible intersectionality. Placing my personal narrative in conversation with the narratives of "strangers" whom I connect with due to our common yet differing subjectivities is an intrinsically political and spiritual practice (Alexander, 2005).
15. See Towle (2009).
16. See National Center for Lesbian Rights (2009).
17. Brandi Rose Hobson (September 20,1983–September 2, 2001), raped and strangled in 2001. Family member of a friend, I invoke a ritual of remembrance (Brown, 2009, p.79).

References

Alexander, J.M. (2005). Pedagogies of crossing: Meditations of feminism, sexual politics, memory and the sacred. Durham, NC: Duke University Press.

Baldwin, J. (1985). The evidence of things not seen. New York: Holt, Rinehart and Winston.

Bambara, T.C. (1980). The salt eaters. New York: Random House.

Brown, R.N. (2009). Black girlhood celebration: Toward a hip-hop feminist pedagogy. New York: Peter Lang

Byrne, J. (2009, September 26). Two cousins dead in west side shooting. Chicago Breaking News Center. Retrieved from: http://articles.chicagobreakingnews.com/2009-09-26/news/28505096_1_percy-day-cousins-high-school-diploma

Castagno, P.C. (2001). New playwriting strategies: A language-based approach to playwriting. New York: Routledge.

Coleman, V.C. (2010, August 11). 8-year-old caught in crossfire & killed playing jump rope in Chicago. Hiphop Wired. Retrieved from http://hiphopwired.com/2010/ 08/11/8-year-old-caught-in-crossfire-amp-killed-playing-jump-rope-in-chicago-33333/

Deming, B. (1974). We cannot live without our lives. New York: Grossman Publishers.

Dolinar, B. (2009, October 20). Why was Kiwane killed? Retrieved from http://socialistworker.org/2009/10/20/why-was-kiwane-killed

Freeman,K. (2008, May 31). Sakia Gunn: When intolerance breeds murder. Retrieved from http://www.bvonlove.com/2008/05/31/sakia-gunn-when-intolerance-breeds-murder/

Gilmore, R.W. (2007). Golden gulag: Prisons, surplus, crisis, and opposition in globalizing. Berkeley: University of California Press.

Gumbs, A.P. (2011). The zen of young money: Being present to the genius of black youth. Crunk Feminist Collective. Retrieved from: http://crunkfeministcollective.wordpress.com/2011/01/24/the-zen-of-young-money-being-present-to-the-genius-of-black-youth/

Hawkins, K. (2009, September 28).Derrion Albert beating death: 4 teens charged with murder. Retrieved from http://www.huffingtonpost.com/2009/09/28/derrion-albert-beating-de_n_302321.html

Lorde, A. (1990). Need: A chorale for black woman voices. Latham, NY: Kitchen Table: Women of Color Press.

Minaj, N. (2011). Moment 4 life.On Pink Friday [CD]. New York: Universal Motown.

National Center for Lesbian Rights. (2009, November 23). Miriam Mercado, mother of Jorge Steven Lopez Mercado, thanks supporters [Video file]. Retrieved from http://nclrights.wordpress.com/2009/11/23/miriam-mercado-mother-of-jorge-steven-lopez-mercado-thanks-supporters/

Standley, F.R., & Pratt, L.H. (Eds.).(1989). Conversations with James Baldwin. Jackson: University of Mississippi Press.

Towle, A. (2009, November 16). Gay Puerto Rican teen decapitated, dismembered, and burned. Retrieved from http://www.towleroad.com/2009/11/gay-puerto-rican-teen-decapitated-dis-membered-and-burned.html

ten

Tasseography as a Healing Practice

Education in a Post-Racial Classroom

Akil Houston

TASSEOGRAPHY TAKE 1

Enclosed in a clenched fist I drop a collection of note cards.

I repeat this action until note cards decorate the carpeted floor of my office.

There it is.

Literary tile. Ready to be laid as the foundation from which to build. However, before building I read.

Silence.

Scribbled on each card are the thoughts, the feelings of students. Pure, undiluted, without edit and without worry of who sees, or who knows what each of them is feeling. The singular prompt is to write about how you feel. So often dialogue in the academy about gender, race, sexual orientation and class is rigid, stiff, cold, predictable.

Not today.

Being comfortable with being uncomfortable.

This act is intentional.

How do you feel?

Write it down.

I see the cards.

No name. Just feelings.

Silence again.

TASSEOGRAPHY TAKE 2

The patterns are forming.

I group the note cards into themes.

"Just cause we have a Black President doesn't mean things have changed, I'm white and I can see that"

"A Black President? Like he got that position because he was so outspoken about race stuff, I don't feel like he really does talk about it, if he does its like almost so quiet like"

"Even though I have white skin I'm *Latino* not Hispanic I don't feel like media shows me"

"You would think that at this school people wouldn't be so caught up with race, but even some of my professors expect me to know all things Black since I'm Black, I feel embarrassed because I don't know I'm just one person"

"I feel like this is the only time a professor asked me what I think and really wanted to know. I feel like there is something that needs to be done but I'm not real sure what I could do. Some kid has a confederate flag in my hall nobody says anything really but somebody ripped down the black history month stuff. My friends think its racist to have black history month. I don't know. I feel like its not but I don't really [know] how to bring it up"

"I hate the race conversation! Nobody cares"

"We need more chances to talk about these issues together, being white, gay and poor, I'm not your typical kid at least not around here"

TASSEOGRAPHY TAKE 3

The cards are now organized around corresponding themes in the next classes reading and screenings. The students feel a personal stake in the conversation because they know what they have to say, and how they feel is an integral part of the class. The screening time is split between conversation, reflection, questioning, and viewing.

Tasseography as a Healing Practice: Education in a Post-Racial Classroom

The post-racial classroom is a space that requires intentional acts by teachers who view education as a practice of freedom. This essay argues that Tasseography is a healing practice. Tasseography is the use of purposeful silence, mediated reflection, and dialogue. The combination of these activities helps students and educators to keep their own feelings in balance with their own thoughts. Bringing this feeling-ness and mindfulness to the classroom is a way that "reveals the human power to make history and culture at the same time that historical and cultural realities shape human experience" (Glass, 2004, p. 17).

How do you do it? This is the question usually asked by students who have taken an introductory media course I facilitate. Most often this question comes some time near the end of the term, or specifically after a class that has had some intense reading and discussion about the intersections of class, race, and gender. The students want to know how it is possible to listen to statements of denial, avoidance, guilt, and anger without "completely losing it," as one student put it. The students who ask this question are passionately curious students, the kind any professor would want to work with. These are people who see class as an opportunity to unlearn, to learn, to question, and—as clichéd as it may seem—to make themselves better people.

The question of how to do it or specifically how I do it is a question I, too, have asked myself numerous times and in numerous ways. This is a question I revisit each year. How do I facilitate a course that engages critical issues in a way that is stimulating, educational, and respectful of the various sites of knowledge students bring to the academic space? In addition, how do I maintain these objectives and meet the necessary missions of the university, college, and department when these areas may be in conflict?

This philosophical and practical question is one that should always be asked when engaging in the art of teaching. Given the current zeitgeist, this question takes on increasing importance. We are living in a time of glaring contradiction. Numerous symbols of progress abound, while the substance of change is less tangible. This is a time in which much of the so called *developed* world, through technology, has some of the most sophisticated forms of communication. Yet much of the world, particularly the so called *developed* world, is lacking in its ability to communicate humanely and has retreated to a technocratic survivalism. A function of this survivalist mentality has also been marked by a reactionary fight opposed to multi-ethnic coalitions and engagement with a wider notion of inclusion and diversity. This is a period where "overt racial discrimination is not as fashionable as it once was" (hooks, 2010, p. 7) yet through thinly veiled rhetoric, racism, sexism, and classism are as prevalent as ever.

While these challenges are not new, *much of this contemporary backdrop has been influenced in part by Tea Party politics and the continued rise of neo-liberal and neo-conservative ideology that fuels* an open attack on progressive educational practice and policy. These dynamics can be seen at work in the Texas School Board of Education's revision of the curriculum to lessen the focus on the Civil Rights Movement and the institution of enslavement. These components are also at play with Florida's Jeb Bush signing into law that "American history shall be viewed as factual, not as constructed" (Jenson, 2006) as well as the "birther movement," which holds that the first African American U.S. president, Barack Obama, is not a U.S. citizen. In universities, according to Giroux (2010b), this takes the form of students being

> urged by some conservative groups to spy on their professors to make sure they do not say anything that might actually get students to think critically about their beliefs. At the same time faculty are being relegated to nontenured positions and because of the lack of tenure, which offers some guarantees, are afraid to say controversial things inside and outside of classrooms for fear of being fired. (pp. 3–4)

As if these factors were not enough, included in this contemporary landscape is the uncertainty of the future. Economic recessions typically result in anxiety. These anxieties produce fear and resentment of the country's marginalized. Instead of seeing their suffering as a symbolic miners' canary, many have retreated to attacking the most vulnerable of society. Institutions of education that have served as a democratic society's safeguard have also been under attack. Educators and teacher unions that oppose budget cuts, tuition hikes, and layoffs, and encourage critical thought and cultural pluralism in classrooms are viewed as selfish or promoting a "non academic" agenda. At the heart of these tensions lies a familiar fear—a fear of a nation that will, more than ever, actually look like the diverse nation it has always been. A 2008 *Washington Post* article forecasts that, collectively, so-called ethnic minorities would become the U.S. majority. "So-called minorities, the Census Bureau projects, will constitute a majority of the nation's children under 18 by 2023 and of working-age Americans by 2039" (Roberts, 2008, p. 1). When this demographic shift takes place, it will signal the end of a single ethnic group as the dominant numerical population. Implied with that shift is the reality of a greater cultural, ethnic, and socially diverse United States. The very idea of greater inclusion, potential of access, and increased diversity means the diminishing of a white-supremacist ideology that dominates much of the framework of education. All of these shifts make for an uneasy transition for those not accustomed to shared power.

Yet before we get there, there must be ways *to* get there. This returns to the question of how do you create and sustain classrooms that challenge racism, sexism, and other variables of inequality when these ideas and practices are imbedded in the dominant ideology? When awareness and critical assessments of institutional disadvantage are viewed as suspect opinions instead of actual forces with empirical data attesting to their existence? In other words, how can educators seek to provide space for academic discourse that addresses significant issues and real-life consequences in a contested space, particularly when the contested space is not only the recognition of the inherent difficulty of this subject matter but a reflection of the ongoing cultural wars that have plagued education in the United States.

Multicultural pedagogy seemed to provide the greatest possibility. However, in many classrooms, it has been hijacked and has provided little more than window-dressing diversity, a kind of diversity that does little to engage students and educators beyond knowing a few more names of communities of color during a Black, women's, or (insert marginalized group's name) month. As the late educational theorist Asa Hilliard (1995) stated:

> There have been many positive attempts over the past few years—human relations, multicultural education, and antiracism workshops and conferences, ethnic studies course development, guidelines to eliminate stereotypes.... However, if we examine the activities conducted under any of these headings, there is a general absence of a historical and theoretical base...in other words, a plan of remedial action should be based upon some knowledge or theory as to what the problem is, how it came about, what maintains it, and how it can be changed. (p. 150)

Hilliard (1995) goes on to explain the challenges of multicultural pedagogy when he notes:

> When a program of multicultural education is launched, what is the precise nature of the problem it attempts to address? Are the problems of privilege and oppression traceable to cultural misunderstanding alone, or are there other causes such as greed, fear, or ideology that make some members of one group attempt to oppress others? If the latter is the case, then one would be hard pressed to explain how training in a particular type of multicultural education addresses the root cause of the problem. (p. 150)

As Hilliard (1995) illustrates, the challenges of this approach lie in the arbitrary nature of application. Although well intentioned, without clear aims and goals it may not produce desired results, or worse, render progressive potential meaningless. What is needed and what I suggest is a practical philosophy of praxis: an approach that responds to an enlightened racism and sexism that surfaces in classroom discourse without being reactionary, or what I am referring to as post-racial resistance to teaching.

Post-racial resistance comes from the belief that the election of Barack Obama has rendered all matters regarding race inconsequential. As a result, society is in a post-racial moment. Therefore, any race-related discourse specifically, and discussions on difference in general, are unnecessary. In classrooms this position is strengthen by popular culture's belief, that enslavement ended and Jim Crow was completely defeated by the Civil Rights Movement. Further, since these activities happened long ago, and there is greater visibility of people of color, race as well as these topics have already been transcended. With the frequency of success stories of African Americans and women such as Oprah, Jay Z, Condoleezza Rice, and Halle Berry, little space is granted to discuss "a more ominous racial condition: capital deficiencies" (Brooks, 2009, p. xii) created by the legacy of Jim Crow. As Roy L. Brooks (2009) notes:

> We hear and read about the racial success stories in the mainstream media, but we hear and read very little about the myriad racial problems black Americans continue to encounter.... In 1974, the percentage of all black families living below the poverty line was about 28%, compared with 6% for all white, non-Hispanic families. In 2004, the black rate decreased by only 7 points to about 21%, whereas the white rate remained unchanged. The median family income for blacks was about $29,000 in 1972 versus about $49,000 for whites, a $20,000 difference. In 2004 the racial difference increased: about $37,000 for black families versus about $63,000 for white families, a difference of $26,000. (p. xii)

A practice in classrooms by both student and teacher is needed that gets to the core of discussing these inequalities. As Dewey, Weems, Green, and other critical theorists have argued, "reaching an epiphany or new understanding about yourself and/or the world is a crucial epistemological element" (Weems, 2003, p. 2). Because of their importance these elements should be nurtured and make up a fundamental component in classroom discourse.

Tasseography emerges as such a practice. Tasseography, as it is traditionally understood and practiced, is a method for stimulating the senses to develop creative solutions. In a classroom context as discussed here it is meant to provide the teacher and the student with a way to hear one's self, the *how to do it* process. Tasseography is purposeful silence, mediated reflection and dialogue. By considering the forces helping to construct and frame certain forms of student ideology, particularly Tea Party rhetoric, tasseography emerges as a way to read the sediments of popular discourse. By understanding how these forces work, it aids in a way to foster interpretations, ideas, and solutions. These are opportune moments of reflection, hearing, and healing. I argue, as Boler (2004) has, that all voices are not equal, and any effort by educators to create a space that is hostility free or comfortable for all is both impossible and impractical. As Boler (2004) asserts, the task is to "challenge oneself and one's students to critically analyze any statements made in a classroom, especially statements that are rooted in dominant ideological values that subordinate on the basis of race, gender, class, or sexual orientation" (p. 4). The goal is not to create a police state in classrooms where all thought, expression, and individuality is muted, but to provide space for those voices, experiences, and people on the margins of discourse.

Tasseography in the Classroom

Suggesting tasseography as an educational philosophical approach may seem strange or odd given common understandings of what tasseography actually is. Tasseography historically is the practice of reading tea leaves or coffee grounds to determine a course of future action. Within the context of classroom dialogue this methodology hardly creates the perception of using class time effectively. Yet Flax (1993) reminds us that

> the world of scholarship/knowledge is a world of freedom populated by individual minds bound only by laws generated by reason itself. This is the world of speech and writing, in which minds speak to themselves and others. In this world all ends can be submitted to critical evaluation as long as the rules of argument, evidence, and consensus-seeking are obeyed. (p. 81)

More than a methods fetish that does little more than respond to a need to have new labels for old ideas and practices, tools are needed that seek to go within the student and the teacher. Approaches that reach across dividing lines and open up communication are of more value than a one-size-fits-all application. The historical use of tasseography already extends across geographical, political, and linguistic borders. Partly responsible for this is "the significance of the ubiquitous, cross cultural and historical pervasiveness of tea, coffee and sediment reading" (TasseographyTasseomancy, 2003–2006), which practitioners of tasseography argue "may be related to the primal human desire for understanding the self " (TasseographyTasseomancy, 2003–2006). Tasseography grew in popularity during the 1830s as a practice of leisure, concurrent with the growth of psychological analysis. "[T]he practice distinguishes itself from…fortune telling, mystical, occult or other magical activities…tasseography is not an application of magic, but rather a tool for tapping into the subconscious by applying meditation to pattern recognition and symbols" (TasseographyTasseomancy, 2003–2006). Jung (1990) reminds us that in our explorations of the human psyche one would

> be better advised to abandon exact science, put away his scholar's gown, bid farewell to his study, and wander with human heart throughout the world. There in the horrors of prisons, lunatic asylums and hospitals, in drab suburban pubs, in brothels and gambling-hells, in the salons of the elegant, the Stock Exchanges, socialist meetings, churches, revivalist gatherings and ecstatic sects, through love and hate, through the experience of passion in every form in his own body, he

would reap richer stores of knowledge than text-books a foot thick could give him, and he will know how to doctor the sick with a real knowledge of the human soul. (pp. 246–247)

Jung is calling on reflection and meditation on the human condition from the various on-the-ground locations where it unfolds, a purposeful introspection. In classroom practice this is the kind of knowledge that is necessary to begin to investigate and analyze problems that cannot be resolved without feelings. This kind of self-reflexive activity is critical in such a paradoxical moment, a moment in the eve of the 21st century in which Barack Obama's presidency signals to some that the notion of a post-racial United States has become a reality. Yet at the same time, this "first" has served as a catalyst for a host of reactionary forces most visibly surfacing as the various numerations of the Tea Party.

While we may like to think the classroom is a place of objectivity—value free education—it is not a neutral space. Teaching is a political act by virtue of what is included and what is not, which voices are heard and which voices are not. "The uniqueness of classrooms is that ideally they provide a public space in which marginalized and silenced voices can respond to ignorant expressions rooted in privilege, white supremacy, or other dominant ideologies" (Boler, 2004, p. 4). Tasseography requires listening, feeling, processing and hearing. This practice requires intentionally creating spaces for marginalized voices. Unless educators are willing to purposefully create opportunities for self-reflection for themselves and their students, they may be unintentionally recreating the status quo in their teaching and teaching space.

The pervasive pedagogy of hate rhetoric masquerading as a fight to restore the country has gained such credibility due to exposure via media outlets and public opinion makers that it becomes challenging for students to critically think for themselves. Attacks on education and the rise of the anti-intellectual have marked what Giroux (2010a) refers to as the disappearing intellectual in the age of economic Darwinism. As Giroux (2010a) notes:

The formative culture, public spheres and institutions capable of challenging this…notion of survivalism…are both under siege and rapidly vanishing. The public intellectual has been replaced by the anti-public intellectual, just as the university as a democratic public sphere is now colonized by corporate and national security interests. Social movements barely speak beyond a narrow identity politics, and the questions that connect agency to pedagogy and social change have been replaced by the search for consumers and clients. (¶ 3)

To constructively challenge this, a return to learning that is inclusive of the imagination-intellect (Weems, 2003) is needed. Tasseography in its purposeful silence, mediated reflection and dialogue seeks to reconnect thoughts with goals, values, and our understanding of the social universe. As Ayers and Alexander

(2010) argue, "The more aware we are of our thoughts and goals, the more we question everything, the more responsible we are for our values and beliefs, the more intentional we can become in creating spaces that speak and work for us" (p. 37).

Being self-aware is not only important in classrooms; it is a critical component to life literacy. Educators must challenge themselves and their students to recognize that "the mere imparting of information is not education. Above all things it should make a [person] think and do for [themselves]" (Woodson, 1933, p. 20). Tasseography is a practice that works within Weems's (2003) imagination-intellect theory. In the discussion of Utopia, Weems identifies five elements that are at the core of imagination-intellect development: aesthetic appreciation, oral expression, written expression, performance, and social consciousness. The practice of tasseography works well with these five core areas, but specifically with oral expression and social consciousness. Oral expression calls for

[a]ssisting students in becoming personally engaged with language through improvisational storytelling, rapping, flowing, hip hop, improvisational skits, debate and public speaking.... Becoming an effective oral performer and/or presenter boosts student self-esteem while helping them develop a valuable ability. (p. 5)

Social consciousness in Weems's (2003) Utopia states that:

Students need to learn an intercultural history, an awareness of their social position in society enabling them to honor diversity, and to put social justice, including the importance of a true participatory democracy, at the forefront. A creative-critical, social consciousness shapes an imagination-intellect capable of envisioning, and actively working toward a better, more humane world. (pp. 5–6)

By infusing tasseography, which is purposeful silence, mediated reflection and dialogue, in these core elements of imagination-intellect development, both students and educators can be more mindful of their own feelings. Being aware of the feelings that construct forms of student ideology is a useful tool in challenging and transforming oppressive practices.

Classroom Reflections

My application of tasseography takes root in African American Studies media courses. I view teaching in African American Studies as a sacred art. As teachers in this discipline "we inherit a great responsibility...for we must give voice to centuries not only of silent bitterness and hate but also of neighborly kindness and sustaining love" (Walker, 1983, p. 22). Tasseography provides an opportunity to engage students. "Engaged pedagogy begins with the assumption that we learn best when there is an interactive relationship between student and teacher" (hooks, 2010, p. 19). By engaging students in dialogue and reflection on issues of difference they must confront their own feelings as well as thoughts on the matter. While this alone does not equate transformation, it is a critical first step in awareness that can lead to transformation. As Gloria Ladson-Billings (2009) states in her study of successful teachers, a strong focus on student learning through the development of a social-political awareness is the cornerstone of success for educators using a variety of methodological approaches.

Though some educators may be ambivalent about creating intentional spaces of silence, mediated reflection and dialogue because of the risks or conflicts, liberatory educators as a practice of education for democracy should be open to the uncomfortable as an example for student openness. It is through such openness that a student left these comments in her reflection (personal communication, 2008) in class:

> I almost didn't come to class today. I thought we would have that class discussion in which race was the big deal it was, but it was different because I felt like I could have my say about how race and class matters and it's not just one thing… it's how they come together…this way we are talking with and not at each other and being heard is better because I feel like at least for me it's not just class. I always felt like this stuff was the other guy's problem…but looking around I realize we are all the other guy and so we all have something to say and at stake.

If educators are invested in education as the practice of liberation, it must be grounded in experiences that seek to heal and create meaningful experiences for themselves and for students. Meaningful interactions can be like the penetrating aroma of tea. Once inhaled, the aroma can create a stimulation of the senses. In an educational sense tasseography is meant to stir our imaginations. Tasseography is a means to reconnect an awareness of the relationship between our feelings, thoughts, and actions. Hopefulness will not provide liberation alone; "hope as an ontological need, demands an anchoring in practice" (Freire, 2004, p. 2). A commitment to honor the significance of feeling, thoughtful reflection and dialogue is a powerful and needed practice.

References

Ayers, W., & Alexander-Tanner, R. (2010) *To teach: The journey in comics.* New York: Teachers College Press.

Boler, M. (2004). All speech is not free: The ethics of "affirmative action pedgagogy." In M. Boler (Ed.), *Democratic dialogue in education: Troubling speech, disturbing silence* (pp. 3–13). New York: Peter Lang.

Brooks, R.L. (2009) *Racial justice in the age of Obama.* Princeton, NJ: Princeton University Press.

Flax, J. (1993). *Disputed subjects: Essays on psychoanalysis, politics and philosophy*. New York: Routledge.

Freire, P. (2004). *Pedagogy of hope: Reliving Pedagogy of the oppressed*. New York: Continuum.

Giroux, H. (2010a) Remembering Howard Zinn. Truthout. Retrieved from http://www.truth-out.org/remembering-howard-zinn-once-again67226

Giroux, H. (2010b). The disappearing intellectual in the age of economic Darwinism. Truthout. Retrieved from http://www.truth-out.org/the-disappearing-intellectual-age-economic-darwinism61287?print

Glass, R. (2004). Moral and political clarity and education as a practice of freedom. In M. Boler (Ed.), *Democratic dialogue in education: Troubling speech, disturbing silence* (pp. 15–32). New York: Peter Lang.

Hilliard, A. (1995). *The maroon within us: Selected essays on African American community socialization*. Baltimore: Black Classic Press.

hooks, b. (2010). *Teaching critical thinking: Practical wisdom*. New York: Routledge.

Jenson, R. (2006). Florida's Fear of History: New Law Undermines Critical Thinking. Retrieved from http://www.commondreams.org/views06/0717-22.htm

Jung, C. (1990). *Two essays on analytic psychology*. Princeton, NJ: Princeton University Press.

Ladson-Billings, G. (2009). *The dreamkeepers: Successful teachers of African American children*. San Francisco, CA: Jossey-Bass.

Roberts, S. (2008, August 13). In a generation, minorities may be the U.S. majority. *The New York Times*. Retrieved from http://www.nytimes.com/2008/08/14/washington/14census.html

TasseographyTasseomancy. (2003–2006). Retrieved from http://www.tasseography.com/history.htm

Walker, A. (1983). *In search of our mothers' gardens: Womanist prose*. New York: Harcourt, Brace, Jovanovich.

Weems, M. (2003). *Public education and the imagination-intellect: I speak from the wound in my mouth*. New York: Peter Lang.

Woodson, C.G. (1933). *The mis-education of the Negro*. Washington, DC: Associated Publishers.

eleven

What Does It Mean to Be a Nigger in the Academy?

Mary E. Weems

Collectively [B]lack people remain rather silent about representations of whiteness in the [B]lack imagination. As in the old days of racial segregation where [B]lack folks learned to "wear the mask," many of us pretend to be comfortable in the face of whiteness only to turn our backs and give expression to   intense levels of discomfort. Especially talked about is the representation of whiteness as terrorizing. Without evoking a simplistic essentialist "us and them" dichotomy that suggests [B]lack folks merely invert stereotypical racist interpretations so that [B]lack becomes synonymous with goodness and white with evil, I want to focus on that representation of whiteness that is not formed in reaction to stereotypes but emerges as a response to the traumatic pain and anguish that remains a consequence of white racist domination....
   —bell hooks (Roediger, 43)

What do you call a Black man with a PhD? Nigger.
   —Malcolm X

Here I use the negative connotation of a word I grew up with, that identifies me and my so-called 'hood origin better than Colored, Negro, Black, Afro-American, and the current African American. A word I snatched from the mouth of the last racist I heard say it, and wrote it in chalk on my forehead so I wouldn't forget him. A word I say with friendship, love, or anger depending upon the situation. In this auto/ethnographic, sacred performance text, I share my lived experience response to being a part-time, then full-time, now part-time professor after teaching at 4 different universities in the last 8 years.

Some may ask: How does this work represent anti-racist struggle? Is there a space for other anti-racists to enter who are looking for ways to act against the institutional racism that, in part, keeps the number of Ph.D.s of color in the academy down? My response to these questions is that the first step toward solving a problem is recognizing its existence. Anti-racists who are looking for ways to counter these situations should consider this piece both an invitation to reach a better understanding of what it think-feels like to be one of the few in the academy; and a challenge to make increasing our numbers part of their individual and collective anti-racist struggle.

"Never doubt that a small group of committed people can change the world. It's the only thing that ever has."
—Margaret Mead

Imaginary Brother on my street: So, miss-sistah-big shit what does it mean to be a nigger professor?

Me (Almost Laughing):

It mean that after making the difficult decision to leave your home, your large family, the city you were born and raised in and everything you love, to move to a small rural, college town. After completing challenging doctoral classes, writing your umpteenth 30-page paper, passing exams, having your dissertation idea accepted, doing your research, completing your draft, revising, revising, revising it, defending it, depositing it like coin in a bank, graduating and finally getting your Ph.D., you first avoid the university like the plague, refuse to say you are a scholar cause the word don't feel right, return to your home cause you want to make a difference in the lives of the Black folks who live where you come from.

It mean that while your degree has the power to, and does open doors for you automatically like magic, while you're able to stand as a positive example for other Black folks you encourage to believe that if you can do it they can too—it's not stamped on your face like a tattoo, so while you have the Black privilege bell hooks writes of, you still a Nigger to any racists you meet.

It mean that after two years of working in k–12 urban public, private, and suburban school after school as an educational consultant—loving it, loving making a positive difference in the lives of young Black kids, white kids, and other kids of color, and their teachers—you feel an obligation to the Black department head where you earned your Ph.D., and to a white woman you love, to give the academy a try.

It mean once you get there, you are always either the only, or one of two—only the brotha or sistah stay so busy being on every committee that say Black, or multicultural, or diversity, teaching, publishing in overwhelmingly white journals, and trying to have some personal life, that you keep in touch by e-mail, and manage to eat lunch together once a month.

It mean you always, always, always are the one who have to get in to fit in—make a place outta no place; feel welcome when few say *come on in.*

It mean you see the same look in some white students eyes every first day of class the good lord send that say: Are *you* the professor?

It mean you are always double checking yourself to make sure you're being as fair as possible, cause you lived what it's like to be treated like shit by a professor yo' damn self—that you always remindin' yourself to remember that white folks, like most k–12 students, don't get too much Black History in school and what they do get is all fucked up. It mean that you can never translate the silence in your classroom without considering whether or not one of your students is thinking "nigger."

It mean you constantly smilin' at white folks in the halls, main office, bathroom, and parking lot who don't know they lookin' at you like you just dropped down from the sky to funk up they atmosphere.

It mean when you teach in a small town and go to the local dermatologist, he tells you he doesn't have any experience with Black skin, then recommends you to some mothafucka in the closest city you rarely have time to drive to:

"Whites Only"

It's in the no-smile, smiles,
bodies that apologize
when you pass by, the lie
on the lips when you cry
about some supposedly
small thing that is the ocean.

It's the notion that we
Are only *hurt* the same
When same = them.
it's changing
the park-place whites walk
when you walk there-it's not
being able to get your hair done
in the small town
where you live

like the last night
with no stars.

It's driving slower in your car
knowing cops are waiting
for you to go 26 instead of 25
miles,
the long-short story
you never get a chance
to tell—the practiced
look of surprise when you do.

It mean when you talk on purpose like you talk when back home, just to hear the sound of your own culture, its cadence moving from comfort to cootie crawl in one syllable, you can't help thinkin' "hope they don't think I'm not intelligent."

It mean you constantly resist the urge to whip out your credentials, cause you think you

need to prove you've earned the right to be there.

It mean no matter how many cool white folks you meet, know, and befriend—you *still* have times you need a white people break bad as hip need hop, so you can let your locs down around people you don't have to explain your feelings to—ya'll can just relax, laugh, cuss, and sigh together.

It mean along with the wonderful white students you have in yo mostly all-white classes, you will always have to read shit written from a position of institutional and/or militant ignorance like: Black men have a extra muscle in they legs and that's why they so good at sports; that they don't think the "one" Black person in their elementary, middle, or high school had any problem being the *only*. That Black people need to get over: slavery, racism, poverty, the kkk, the nice-white-racists, the police—that Black people "have" overcome and the ones still struggling are lazy—shit that hurts until you get used to it—and you don't.

It means you watch films, and read books and have discussions about the Black experience, re-visiting wounds in places in your spirit that can't rest. It mean you "are" the Black experience for too, too many of your students, and it's like trying to teach a foreign language to elders.

It mean that when you talk about caring, sharing, respecting, and learning from each other, that you can't think without feeling at the same time, you have students who feel comfortable cheating on your dramatic performance midterm, then sending you e-mails accusing you of grading them according to a "voodoo formula" they're "not privy to."

It mean that sometime you feel so low to the ground, you get real quiet, go home and spend a weekend in bed alone because your man, your life-partner lives somewhere else—crying until your tears are dirt.

* * *

Tuesday, November 2, 2004, a white male student in an English composition course I'm teaching informed me that "I'm not the kind of professor he can learn from," and that because of my teaching style, which is centered in establishing community, student responsibility for their educative experience, mutual respect, reciprocal learning, and sharing—he has learned absolutely nothing in my class since the semester began.

After giving yet another university my best effort, as a part-time professor, I'm questioning my spiritual ability to remain inside its overwhelmingly ivory tower. I'm asking myself if real, enduring, powerful social change is ever gon' come. If making the small difference I've been able to make is worth the constant reminder, along with the positive things that occur, that in the end, in the silence of the white majority—I'm *still* just another Nigger in the academy.

Postscript

It's been almost 7 years since I wrote this piece. In revisiting my words, I consider them in light of my current position as a full-time, tenure-track faculty member who has sought and become part of a community of colleagues both in and outside my department. I critically consider what, if anything has changed about the institutionalized racism of the academy. Based upon my own experiences and ongoing conversations with Black colleagues and other colleagues of color in the United States and other parts of the world, I conclude that like my uncle Jack used to say about the streets, the only thing that's changed with any degree of significance are the faces of the players; the racist, white, ivory tower remains the same.

References

Roediger, D.R. (Ed.) (1998). *Black on white: Black writers on what it means to be white.* New York: Schocken.

twelve

Migrant Stories
Searching for Healing in Autoethnographies of Diaspora

Marcelo Diversi and Claudio Moreira

I am
We are the
Borders we cross
The places we live and labor

* * *

How Far from Where We Fall In?

As migrating human beings, we find our very existence, simple as they are in the larger scheme of things, constantly being represented as the Other, the different, the outsider, the foreigner, the accented, not part of Us, part of Them, and seldom in a kind way. Right, wrong, in between, or both, we believe this is a common experience of a large part of the billions in the human kind. And who isn't directly related to someone from someplace else?

How far from the spot on which we plop upon arrival till we qualify as a migrant on this planet?

Ten feet to the washing basin?

Ten miles to school?

Tens of borders away from your first place on earth?

How far from where we first touch the earth till we can justify the exclusion of fellow human beings on the fleeting base of belonging to a land?

That assumes, beyond all reason

And kindness,

That any chunk of land can belong to any of us

Till "us" means everyone.

* * *

Learning English

The year is 1999. I am in my reading English class. The teacher is introducing new words in our limited vocabulary in English. It is a basic exercise. The teacher reads the word aloud and we, the students, try to guess the meaning.

"Alien" the teacher says

I raise my hand very fast. I know the word.

"Claudio, go ahead."

"Monster! Alien is a monster!" I say with confidence…

Dan, the teacher has a funny smile in his face.

"A monster? Are you sure, Claudio?"

"Yes, I watched the movie…with Sigourney…can't pronounce her name…"

Dan is still wearing his smile

"Yes Claudio, it may be a monster like in the movie, but it is also you."

"Me????? I am not that thing! I am a human being."

* * *

Local Immigrants

I've recently moved to a new community. Once again, I've encountered the familiar things of life in a new place: not knowing where to go for food, not knowing anyone to ask. New streets, new blind spots, new local corks. This newness has always been more pleasure than pain for me. Even getting lost in a new city is appealing to me, like an adventure with few serious threats beyond other human beings. Needless to say, I have been lucky to move to places I've chosen, always with privileged resources and back-up plans.

But I've always felt a bit bad about arriving with suitcases. New cities are already too crowded. People all around seem to know where they are going. Young, old, and otherwise appear to carry on with a sense of familiarity I don't have. I can't suppress the feeling that I am butting in, invading their land, one more body in line, interrupting their daily bustle with questions about the obvious. Excuse me sir, ma'am, where is the post office? A simple question like that is often enough for the immediate establishment of a dualistic relationship of Us and Them, insider and outsider, local and migrant. The tension rests on how the local responds to the sudden recognition of a migrant.

This time, I was moving to an allegedly progressive place, the Pacific Northwest. I wasn't sure what my friends meant by "progressive," but I must have imagined, uncritically, some notion about this being a more inclusive community. At the more conscious level, I knew Pacific Northwesterners were, well, people. But somewhere between consciousness and daydreaming I thought that everyone I saw walking around in my new community brewed their own beer, ate veggies from their own organic communal garden, raised urban chickens for hormone and cruelty-free eggs, drove hybrids with Free Tibet bumper stickers, but only when their bicycles were getting tuned up at the co-op around the corner. I bought my first COEXIST t-shirt at the local farmer's market and hoped it made for a good cover.

Then I went to my new faculty orientation. I felt strangely at home as soon as I heard the first statement, a heartfelt welcome to the "Coug family," and a joke about how the joy of being a Coug was heightened by the disastrous year the Huskies had had. Hearty laughter all around. The room felt warmer. Alliances were clear. I hadn't known who the Huskies were until that very moment. But the "them" was framed so incisively that I immediately knew it had to be my university's main competitor in the legislature, the mightier University of Washington.

In no time I started hearing other local us-versus-themisms that grabbed my migrant attention: Washington residents have repeatedly voted against a light-rail line across the Columbia River, a mass transportation option that would greatly improve the quality of living of tens of thousands of Washington residents who fight the brutal bottleneck of the two bridges into Portland, where they work. According to *The Columbian*, the local newspaper, the number one reason for the "no" vote has been the same each time: Washington residents don't want "them," Portlanders, bringing their tattoos, piercings, colored hairdos, queerness, and, God forbid, their tree-hugging tendencies over to "our" side, the good side.

Like in the rest of the country, immigration is a vivid site of us-versus-them discourse in my new community. Latinos are competing with "our" kids for the already scarce school resources. Russians are doing the same, but by *not* sending "their" kids to school. Fellow Americans moving from other states bring "their" liberal ideas and drive prices out of range for "our" families.

Much of this resentment is shared openly and in the self-righteous tones of those who have long forgotten their own migrant journey here. Lewis and Clark are celebrated for opening a migration path to the region for "their" ancestors, the migrant ancestors of the local people.

The centerpiece of the downtown park in my new community is a stylized totem pole honoring the indigenous people who first welcomed Lewis and Clark in 1804. I stood facing the totem pole that first day at the park, listening to the recorded sage-sounding voice coming out of it, accompanied by faint drum beats, a voice that described the importance of the salmon swimming up and down the Columbia River for the many tribes that lived at its margins for thousands of years. Not too far away from the totem pole is a bronze statue of the European soldier who founded the town in 1825. His name was George Vancouver. I could see George from the same spot I stood listening to the totem pole speak and rolled my eyes.

And HOW could I NOT roll my eyes before such sad irony? It's like a Thanksgiving déjà vu, West Coast version. Now that they are no longer part of the troubling "them," the native can be celebrated as part of "us," part of "our" heritage, the generous people who shared turkey and salmon with "us" when "we" needed the most.

I roll my eyes and shake my head. How can "they" be so hypocritical and not even see it?!

And then, I hear it. "They?" I hear my own voice echoing inside my head.

Ah, the chill of catching oneself in that act. The chill of catching MYself being indignant about "their" hypocritical display of us-versus-themism!

I recover my balance between acceptance of what I believe is an inseparable part of my human condition, that is, seeing the world in simpler categories whenever possible, and a renewed desire to further explore ways in which we can develop educational systems that bring a Freirean level of conscientização to mind more easily. If we can't get rid of dualistic tendencies, as I believe, may we at least find ways to be better at identifying it in ourselves, in our so called decolonizing acts. *Before* we try to decolonize others.

* * *

Monsters, Kind Of
I am not that monster am I?
I am a human being am I not?
I am
We are the
Borders we cross
The place we live and labor

I want to teach English in Arizona
I am the hybrid monster/human
The Alien in Sigourney Weaver / Warrant Officer Ripley's womb
Do I look illegal to you?

* * *

"…the real question about the utility of the old Platonic dualisms is whether or not their deployment weakens our sense of human solidarity. I read Dewey as saying that discarding these dualisms will help bring us together, by enabling us to realize that trust, social cooperation and social hope are where our humanity begins and ends" (Rorty, 1999, p. xv)

* * *

Fellow Brazilians
I am going to vote. In the Left of course. I vote for Dilma!
You should not vote, especially for her! You don't live here! You have no right!
Outsider!
Traitor!
If you care that much why you don't fucking live here?
Many answers…
I don't know!

* * *

Bodies and Borders, Body as Border
Moving bodies diasporic
Invading the Brazilian Dream of a melting pot of foreign stock harmony in America!

* * *

Well-Intentioned Essentializing Assumptions of Immigrants
"You should be very proud of yourself," a friendly student recently told me as we walked through the quad after class.
    What do you mean?" I ask a bit surprised.
    "Well, look at you, you came a long way from the tough hand you were dealt. And now you are a college professor in America," he says with a light squeeze of my arm.
    "Tough hand I was dealt?" I ask.

"Yeah, growing up in, er…, the Third World and all," he says.

"It's nice of you to offer this compliment. But I can't accept it in good conscience…"

"I don't mean any disrespect, I promise," he says interrupting me and suddenly looking a bit nervous.

"No offense taken, please, don't worry," I add quickly, "it's just that I had a very privileged upbringing in Brazil, attending high-quality private schools all the way up to college, living with great comfort, supported by a thoughtful and supportive family, lacking for nothing. I got handed an easy hand, truly. Don't you remember me talking about all this on the first day of class? I remember you being there."

"Uh, now that you mention it, I do…but I guess my image of the Third World trumped what you said that day…sorry," he says, looking a bit dejected. Or embarrassed. I can't really tell.

"Active listening can be hard," I say, trying to make a hook with a concept we discussed in a recent class on communicative strategies, trying to let him off the other hook.

We part with a good handshake and smiles. I am glad we got a chance to have this exchange. I should make a greater effort to position my Brazilian upbringing in relation to my students' assumptions about Brazil in particular, and the Third World in general. I should also share some of my own mis-assumptions of Others as an attempt to create narratives of commonality in our struggles to overcome binary linguistic traps of us-themisms.

Isn't that the only way we come to empathize with Others?

By finally being able to see ourselves in the Other's shoes?

Perhaps, I wonder as I walk back to my office, Steve will pause to ponder alternative possibilities of identity next time he meets someone from the Third World. And I sure hope I will carry the memories of this encounter next time I have uncritical impulses to essentialize my own Others.

Possibilities…

* * *

The Hybrid Monster/Human

I

The Alien in Sigourney Weaver / Warrant Officer Ripley's womb

May be not

It may be my English teacher is right after all…were I to be that monster, people in the only America would understand me/us fellow migrants. Were I that monster, violent, cruel, and powerful, America would get us…respect us. The language of violence is clearly understood by the big bully in the world. Violence is the universal language of the empire.

However,

We still are that kind of monster or maybe

Another kind

Hybrid monster/human product of colonial rape

Betweeners

Not violent for sure unless when we use our embodied words

The words are accusatory for sure but only of the system that insists on carnal narratives strong accent, lack of intelligence and work ethic

Lack of loyalty to Country and family and gratitude to the American way of life all mixed in a humungous state of dumbness

Surprise: we're not that dumb

Some of us are poor

Some of us can pass—keep your mouth shut

Some of us Brown, Black, kinda White, Pardo,

Or borrowing from Gloria Anzaldua in her vision of "El Mundo Zurdo"—The Left Hand World.

"Some of us are leftists, some of us practitioners of magic. Some of us are both." (Moraga & Anzaldua, 1981, p. 209)

Some of us are

Our people

Your maids, drivers, caretakers, workers, killers, thieves, robbers, refugees

And even if for a few times,

Your teachers…not being productive and drinking the government milk

Being…such lazy asses

We are not scary, are we?

Were we ripping off people from their own

STOMACH

Not in the belly of the beast but

The Beast in the belly

Killing whatever is in front of us along the way we would at least be

Understood if not respected, even if it comes by fear

Isn't that what America does to the

Other?

Killing and chaos in other places

Vietnam and other places in Asia, Middle East, South and Central America, Western Europe.

* * *

"The title 'Hope in Place of Knowledge' is a way of suggesting that Plato and Aristotle were wrong in thinking that humankind's most distinctive and praiseworthy capacity is to know things as they really are—to penetrate behind appearance to reality. That claim saddles us with the unfortunate appearance-reality distinction and with metaphysics: a distinction, and a discipline, which pragmatism shows us how to do without. I want to demote the quest for knowledge from the status of end-in-itself to that of one more means toward greater human happiness." (Rorty, 1999, p. xiii)

* * *

Why We Left?

Why did we leave our "home" country?

Growing up poor in Brazil is not a good

Thing

I've been in the USA for almost 12 years, all of them as a visa holder. Especially after the "Patriotic Act," as a visa carrier, I have no rights whatsoever, and yet... Citizenship is a concept I experience in the US. I could not vote for Obama as I did for Dilma and yet

My whole life in Brasil was marked by disdain, a third class kinda person not ever, not

Ever

Not once a citizen.

I was 10 or 11 and worked illegally in Brasil. I got paid half of the minimum wage!

Always

Half of the minimum

Half of self

Half of person

Half of being

Yet a whole monster

That kind of monster

With feelings of…gratitude!

As Grandma usually reminded me:

"You got a job; thousands don't."

Gratitude? Just kiss my beautiful behind!

Why I left?

We're the monsters there…not much difference after all. Don't trust me? Go ahead and ask any illegal Bolivian living in São Paulo City. Try this and then tell how their stories differ from the illegal here in this country.

São Paulo and New York, the same side of a different coin!

* * *

Toward Narratives of Healing and Social Hope

We experience life in-between cultures, ethnicities, class, and indigenousness. In Brazil, where we grew up and now go back to for family and research, we are white. In the USA, where we live and labor, we are brown, at least off-white. In Brazil, we are often treated as migrants who have chosen to leave their country of origin and are, at best, outsiders. In the heat of an argument with friends and family about politics, we are called traitors for having left the motherland. In the USA, we are often treated as migrants with a deficit in language, intelligence, and loyalty to country and family. Sometimes we are treated worse, of course. But who isn't? And who doesn't treat others worse than we could? We know we don't have a privileged vantage point on this.

But we speak from a common vantage point, the migrant vantage point. We speak as migrants who weren't migrants until the beginning of our adult lives. We speak as migrants who didn't think much about migrants until we felt the insufferable arrogance and hypocrisy of locals. We speak as migrants who are trying to face our own migrantphobias in the mirror.

"You are welcome to my country!" we have heard from locals who appear to be trying to express warmth and friendship. But these parochial greeters can't see the appalling divisiveness in the gesture. The relationship is immediately gelled into an Us/Them opposition, where the differences are elevated as the relational parameters. And important commonalities vanish in the background. The benign local who shares words of welcome, words that in their very utterance claim higher rights of belonging at the expense of another's basic human right to feel at home anywhere on the planet, positions himself (we have only had men say this to us) as the unalienable owner of the land where we now stand. It's a backdoor reminder that migrants don't enjoy the same rights as locals. To ask such locals whether they, also, were greeted by the previous locals upon their migrant arrival would be too impolite for our taste. So we turn our gaze and critique toward larger structures and narratives that make it possible for this historical forgetfulness to be so ingrained in the sociological imagination in the first place.

While we can do wondrous things in the 21st century, we are still largely deprived of narratives of possibilities for human connection. We are starved for narratives of inclusion so powerful that over time they become more appealing than narratives of exclusion. New Americans instead of legal aliens or foreign stock, say.

We realize this experience of life in-between, where exclusion is too frequent for comfort, isn't unique to us. And we believe that autoethnographies of immigration can be used as a site of possibilities for narratives of life in-between local and foreign. We offer these thoughts as a way of resisting the persistent colonizing discourse about the Other. As a way of seeking healing through emotional connection with the Other through narratives that resonate with each of our own migrant experiences of the world. We believe autoethnographies of immigration can offer readers glimpses into Others' lives that bridge common human experiences of wanting to improve our lot, to belong to larger groups and larger causes, to live meaningful lives. Glimpses that create visceral connection with Others because you could see yourself in the Others' shoes, if only for a brief instant. We attempt to write narratives where the circle of Us becomes more inclusive and the circle of Them becomes harder to justify.

We share autoethnographies of our encounters with the many forces and identities of immigration, both inclusive and exclusionary, with the explicit intent to resist and trouble the persistent single story of the outsider. This single story has been told, particularly in formal education, from the arrogant pedestal of self-proclaimed expertise. It's a view from everywhere, or from objectivity, as the single story experts claim. In our view as accidental immigrants, this theoretical expertise of the Other, of the immigrant, is toxic and exclusionary, regardless of the expert's ethical protestations to the contrary. In the spirit of resistance against ideologies of domination via theoretical expertise and of healing through shared narratives of life as betweeners, we stand on the shoulders of inclusionary performers to try and create representational mirrors of our own encounter with Diaspora—situated, subjective, and partial.

Just as encounters with the Other always are.
We are not erasing the history of forced migration
Slavery, refugees, to name a few
Nor are we sugarcoating the bloodbath of colonial rape
In bodies of color
Nor trying to clean the sanguine fluid in the hands of the white European man
Nor turning a blind eye to the imperialistic project of corporations
The new colonial force of our times
Disguised as Corporations promoting "free" trade
While pushing indigenous peoples out of their homelands
Invariably run by modern Conquistadores

Diaspora always includes some kind of loss
Home, land, identities…
Instead we gain Dark Red memories
Blood
Bodies

But We are dangerous to power! (Madison, 2009) And
Like Gloria Anzaldua (1987), we ask to be met halfway
There, we may have a dialogue
In the halfway place
We must find
Ways
To realize we
Are all
Migrant locals
On this planet
Rise up!

References

Anzaldua, G.E. (1987). *Borderlands: The new mestiza = La frontera* (1st ed.). San Francisco, CA: Aunt Lute Books.

Madison, D.S. (2009). Dangerous ethnography. In N. Denzin & M.D. Giardina (Eds.), *Qualitative inquiry and social justice: Toward a politics of hope*. Walnut Creek, CA: Left Coast Press.

Moraga, C., & Anzaldua, G. (1981). *This bridge called my back: Writings by radical women of color*. Watertown, MA: Persephone Press.

Rorty, R. (1999). *Philosophy and social hope*. New York: Penguin.

thirteen

In Trouble

Desire, Deleuze, and the Middle-Aged Man

Jonathan Wyatt

Lincoln's Castle Hotel lies at the top of Steep Hill in the shadow of the gothic cathedral. Earlier today, when it had been quiet, the hotel's bartender had noticed the man sitting at the corner table. To her, he'd seemed sad, alone with his blue notebook and silver pen. He'd smiled when he approached the bar to ask for a pint of Trout Tickler—"It has to be. It's the name," he'd said—and in the light she'd noticed the lines around his eyes and his hair greying at the side. Older than she'd thought.

"How's the writing?", she'd asked.

"Oh, you know. Slow. I'm better at intending to write than writing." He'd smiled once more as she handed him the glass of the rich, chocolatey brew, then thanked her and returned to his seat.

It was now mid-afternoon. Wedding guests were gathering. She heard the onrush of chattering voices, conversations she found impossible to hear. The emptiness and disposability of words. As she prepared drinks for one—a curt, overdressed woman—she heard the sound of a baby out of sight behind the back of a black leather sofa. It was trying to decide whether or not to cry.

She forgot about the writer, if that's what he was.

* * *

If I were ever sure or stable, I am not now. I am uncertain even who this is that's writing, "threatened...with false steps and false words" (Cixous, 1991, p. 114). One narrative is that I am a man who will soon be 50, and I am in trouble.

I work as a therapist at a doctor's surgery for one day of my working week. I sit with men as their lives jar in mid-life (however defined); men like Jed, Peter, and Michael. They're just names here, but I am writing about us, fifty-ish men, *"(n)el mezzo del cammin di nostra vita"*[1] (Dante, 1975). These stories are both mine and theirs, acts of imagination that (e)merge with experience (Clough, 1995). I do not seek truths—I have no sense of what such things might be—but only the possibilities and impossibilities that might challenge them (Jackson & Mazzei, 2008).

Here, below the ribs at the front. That's where it hurts. Not sharp, but there. Always there.

An affective ache.

When I awake. As I fall asleep. When I make coffee, stack the dishwasher, extend the same seat each morning on the bus. When I discuss the painting of the fascias with Glenn, who's smartening the back of the house. As I reach up the ladder to pass him a mug of tea; milk, one sugar.

"Is that varnish you've used on the wood?", Glenn asks.

I don't know. I don't remember. The substance was translucent ochre, its odour redolent of school cricket pavilions in early summer.

I can be distracted—by Glenn, perhaps—but when I am back in my body it's still there. Some people talk about a 'dull' ache but it's not that. It doesn't bore me: it bores into me, impelled towards my heart, demanding a response.

"Is that glass dead?", the bar girl interrupts, reaching across.

"Yes. Thanks." She leans forward and I glimpse. Looking up, I say, "You're busy now".

"You too, it seems. Keep at it," and moves to the next table.

I use the term "ache" for this pain; I name its place, "below the ribs." Attempts at precision. But neither name nor location are sufficient. I have lost interest, dismissive and intolerant of myself. I don't know what "it" is. I wish it would go away. I tell myself to get a grip.

This is an investigation into uncertainty, an inquiry into the enigma of impulses (Butler, 2005). Partial stories of the ambivalence, the doubt, that middle age is bringing me.

What to Do with Becoming a Cliché

Maybe mine is a straightforward tale of middle-class, middle-aged, middle-England, straight, male, professional, privileged, Western melancholy. This is the blunt, chronological narrative:

Today is July 10, 2010.

In June, our son left university. We beamed on the serried seats in the ancient hall as he collected his degree.

In early July, our daughter left school.

In late July, we will finish paying for our house.

On September 13th I will be 50.

Next year I will have been married for 25 years.

In May, I was drawn to an attractive, intelligent, feisty woman, a few years younger than me.

* * *

A story I could tell:
   After leaving work I walked to the offbeat café and took one of the newspapers, fixed to a wooden rod hanging on the wall, back to the table. I sat by the long window onto the street. "May" did not arrive at the agreed time; I did not take in the football report my eyes passed over. Feigning nonchalance, I carried on reading, then saw her out of the corner of my eye as she walked past the window. No matter how I tried I couldn't help but feel anxious. We greeted each other with a kiss to the cheek. I liked that brief, faint touch. I watched her as she stood in line for coffee. I noticed the way she stood, one be-denimed leg slightly bent, and her hair—how there seemed so much of it but how it seemed to rest lightly on her shoulders. It seemed so bright; neither blonde, nor red, but something of both.
   "There," she said as she placed her coffee on the table and sat down. "Now, how are you?"
   "Fine." A pause. "Yes, fine." Now was not the time. I didn't even know whether there was going to be a time, whether or not I could bring myself to tell her. My anxiety grew.
   We talked about our work, my holiday, her friends; finished our drinks. Then we parted.

* * *

Recognisable, familiar; tame, perhaps. Men reach 50 (and/or 35 and/or 40, and/or whenever), are confronted by the inevitable intimations of mortality, and indulge their mid-life angst. They buy Harley Davidsons, dye their hair, acquire piercings, complete triathlons, become depressed, go paragliding and/or, if the opportunity arises, sleep with younger people. The stuff of comedy and snide laughter; and in some cases, loss, regret, tragedy.

A cliché.

A cliché is banal, over-familiar, well-worn.

Like loss. Like love. They cease to be clichés when given life by the immediacy of the person in the room and the uniqueness of skin, hair, breath, voice. It is not a cliché when it's happening to me.

I spoke with Jay last week. We've done this for 30 years: meet, eat, drink, catch up. We talk about books and writing, film and families; and—still—about the girl at school with whom we, along with most of our contemporaries, were in love. Always, we talk about football. Jay was much the better player, full of feints and twists and subtle skill. We meet on occasions through the year, in the same prosperous but dull middle England town half way between our respective cities. Occasionally we travel to watch a game or, once every few years, bring the families together; but, with children now all but living their own lives, such gatherings are no longer likely. As always, Jay heard my stories. I showed him where it hurt, pointed to the spot, just below the ribs, and he teased me, kindly. The teasing helped. When I sensed I'd taken up too much time I asked him how he was. He laughed and told me that my pain was more interesting. But later, as we walked to the station, he mentioned the heaviness he feels; and how, these days, he feels invisible.

For Jaques (1965), in one well-established take on the psychodynamic narrative of the "mid-life crisis," both men and women become confronted by the inevitable and have to find a way to negotiate, more or less destructively, mourning lost youth. In Erikson's (1959) terms, they are at the seventh stage of life, middle adulthood, questioning meaning and purpose. The perception of life extending ahead indefinitely is no longer sustainable. The end, though maybe distant, is in sight. We face loss, with hope only arising from acceptance and wisdom from embracing the inexorable.

The problem with this neat, compelling interpretation is in its sidelining of the cultural, gendered nuances at play in favour of an essentialist understanding of developmental processes. Without denying the biological shifts, the way the body writes ageing, the cultural scripts are powerful. Men and women both, created and constrained—if not bound—by discourses.

There might be some elements of the disturbances—however experienced, whatever the manifestations—that need attending to. Maybe acceptance isn't possible. Maybe "mid-life" is a crisis that springs from something other than being "a stage" to be passed through. Maybe something is up. (Indeed.) Mid-life may be a *stage*: set for action and performance.

The wedding must be starting soon, she thought. The crowd was thinning and she was taking a chance to draw breath. The baby, who'd been passed round amongst the cluster of guests by the sofa and been pacified, was now being levered into her coat and had begun to complain again. That man was still there, she noticed, writing. Strange, she thought. Why's he on his own? What would make him want to write like that? She'd noticed his looking when she'd stretched to pick up his glass. He'd been discreet, as if it were an accident.

He was looking at, but seemingly not seeing, the cluster of tight-suited men as they placed their empties on his table before turning to leave.

Waking Dreams

There is movement: a haze of bags being searched for, companions being summoned, signals exchanged with the tap of fingers to wrists. The snapshots of these scenes transport me, like waking dreams:

I see the young, self-conscious woman over there, by the fireplace, turning to pick up her jacket—

And I am taken to my 18-year-old daughter leaving with a friend for Ibitha on her first independent holiday. They have only a flight booked and a vague plan that the 28-year-old son of the friend's father's new partner will meet them at the airport. He will, I am assured, look after them and help them find accommodation. She tells me not to worry. She assures me she's sensible. I say, it's not you who worries me.

A group of twenty-something men at the end of the bar, cousins perhaps, hair gelled, still drinking, being harried by parents—

And I hear my twenty-something son asking, a few days ago, how about going for a pint, Dad? I say no. I'm not feeling up to it. (He's home for a month, post-university, pre-travelling.) Yes, that's why I'm asking you, he insists. The walk involves my jogging to keep up with him. How come he walks so fast? I've never understood that. He buys the first drinks (mine a beer, his a Jack Daniels and coke) and we sit outside under the gazebo. He wants to talk and I find I can listen. I offer what I think will be wise words, but he starts to grin: the baby at the table behind my right shoulder is laughing at him as she stands upon her father's lap. Later, as we finish our second drinks, he confides,

"One of my friends asked me how I got on with my parents. I said that my dad was one of my best friends."

I could hug him. I could cry. I touch him on his shoulder and thank him. We walk home.

A small boy, in his smart trousers and a clean t-shirt with the face of a cat, runs a model train between the empty glasses on an empty table—

In the clear bright warmth of Chicago, on South La Salle Street, as the train snaps its rhythm on the raised track of the "L" above us, I disclose to my two friends that I sometimes imagine that when I get old my loss of verbal inhibition will be such that I shall tell those closest to me what I really think. The inner censor's grip will be loosened by dementia or some such disturbance, and my words will hurt because they will be unkind and heartfelt. One responds,

"So, what is it that you are not saying to us that you want to say?"

I am left to wonder what I am holding onto so tight, what it is I fear, what it is I need to connect with.

There's a sign, in gold lettering, above the tall, elderly man looking impatient to leave for the wedding. The sign points guests towards the hotel pool and gym—

I have been going to a gym ever since, two years ago, my right calf rebelled at playing football. After all this time, the right calf no longer tears. I can do 70 single leg calf raises, more than I should rightly need; I can extend the main gastrocnemius muscle and the equally important but hidden soleus on each leg till my shin is less than 45 degrees to my planted foot. I have gradually built up the time that I can run: at first just one minute running followed by one minute walking, repeat five times; then two minutes running, one minute walking, repeat five times; three and one; four and one; and so on until I can now run a full twenty minutes and more. I have hopped, skipped, and jumped on the wooden floor of the small studio, watching in the mirror my ungainly leaps and stumbles.

Painstaking, with many setbacks on the way, usually when, in my complacency or enthusiasm to be well, I've pushed too hard or run too long. I've done everything the physiotherapist has advised me to do. Within the last month I have begun to play football again. The right calf has borne up well. But the left one, having been untroubled all this while, has rebelled and I have to begin all over again.

When I first went to the doctor about my calf he told me, "Jonathan, it's the difference between lamb and mutton, I'm afraid."

I haven't been back.

A voice to the right calls "Adele! Come on!" and a tanned, thirty-something woman some distance away, talking, waves an irritated hand without turning—

My tanned daughter returns from Ibitha. She shows us photographs of her and her friend, both of them smiling and beautiful. She had an exhausting, wonderful time and didn't go to sleep before dawn each night/day. She sports a new tattoo, a rose, on her side.

The little boy, clutching his train, is scooped up tenderly by his mother—

Looking for tenderness, I went for Reiki with Barbara. In the cool of her room, she sat with me. Before we began she asked what I would like to tell her by way of context. I said I was troubled.

"You may not know how this works," she reassured me, "but it might help. I know it's not what you're used to: not everything has to be verbalised."

Laid on the couch, I sensed her hands on me even when they were not; and as I drifted into and away from the room I lost her but knew she was with me, somewhere. When she cupped her hands on my chest, I wanted to hold them. Afterwards, I told her that it was the touch, and the recognition it conveyed, that I had most appreciated.

The elderly man, joined by his wife, turns and walks slowly. He uses a stick—

I think about my father. I don't remember his being this way at 50, but then I wouldn't have noticed. I wonder how he would have been. I think he would have bitten his lip and said nothing, done nothing different, got on with it. I doubt my mother would have known if he had struggled.

One evening last month I slumped, frustrated, into the sofa after a long and irritating phone call about insurance, in which I had been forced to work through endless menus and then a "please hold." I had to sit through more Vivaldi. Relieved it was done, I sat in front of the TV, using the remote control. My right thumb began to shake. A slight, uncontrollable tremor. It continued for minutes. I could not make it stop. A jolt: Parkinson's (see Wyatt, 2005, 2008, etc.). This must have been how Dad first noticed his wrist; what first, in his fifties, must have given him cause for concern. An aberration suddenly present.

I remembered that for half an hour I had been clutching a telephone handset in my right hand. The tremor eased.

The bartender—what's her name? Should I ask?—is being given instructions by her manager, while they clear the counter—

My work colleagues notice that something isn't right. A week ago, one, seizing the opportunity of a quiet moment as people called and laughed outside my office, asked how I was. I enquired why she asked. She told me that she and the others had noticed that I was not quite *with* them, that I seemed absent. At lunch, I took the risk of telling them.

"I'm struggling, I'm not sure why, but I feel such grief. Here."

And held myself just below my ribs. I apologised if I was not on my game and asked them to let me know if they needed something from me that I wasn't giving. They told me it was fine to talk if I wanted. I was touched but knew that I wouldn't.

All the wedding guests are moving towards the door of the hotel. In an hour's time a young couple will be spliced—

Last month, an uncle and aunt celebrated turning 80 and being married 50 years. He stood at the barbecue to speak to family members gathered in the narrow rectangle of urban garden. He told a story during which he mimicked her voice; she feigned protest, eyes down, a coded, intimate, smile. As I stood with other in-laws on the grass, half-empty champagne glass in hand, laughing along with the others, I was aware both of my envy and of an indeterminate dread.

"You must be done now," she quips as she walks past.

"Well, it's just notes at this stage." She stops. "Just some stories and some thinking aloud. I'm getting somewhere though."

"Are you? That's good."

"Well, no, I'm lying. I'm not sure that I am."

She is standing with what must be ten glasses stacked between her right hand on top and her left underneath, and a bar towel over her shoulder. I look around. I'm one of two people still here.

"What's the writing, anyway?"

"It's about being 50, about being a middle-aged git."

"You don't look it."

"What, don't look 50 or don't look a git? Anyway, you're very kind. Thank you."

She says: "I'm finishing shortly."

I reply: "Oh, right. I'll get one more beer before you go."

Questions of Desire

I see a mentor through work. I talk with her about the changes taking place within my organisation, how my friend is leaving and how I will be taking on greater responsibility. I explain how the therapeutic service I work for has become the unquestioning servant to the infallible god of "evidence-based medicine" and how I no longer belong.

She draws with coloured pens a diagram on large paper. It shows a curve that travels down, runs along the bottom, and then up. I am on the downward curve, signifying that I am in the process of becoming aware of the extent of my disruption. I have a choice, either to stay with it to see where it takes me or to fly from it by falling back on established ways of making sense.

She asks me, "What is the nature of your desire?"

I take it as rhetorical and don't answer. She proposes the need for a radical shift in understanding my role. She does not mean only at work. She suggests that English, white culture does not mark transitions well, and that part of my process might be the need to mark a shift into the role of "elder." I want to race through the dark corridors and out into the London afternoon.

That place, below the ribs, just there, where I can touch it, speaks not only of grief. A grief I do not understand. I can identify losses—my father's death, family illness—but none of them seems to suggest this shape and texture. When I place my fingers there, above my belly, feeling the muscles moving with my breath, the fingers sinking slightly into the flesh, seeking out the body's voices, listening, the fingers hear one that sings of longing.

I yearn for May; to be near, beside her, tracing fingers over clear, pale skin; breathing her in, sensing her hair on my shoulder; to be against, pressing, together, hearing her breath, moving with her. I dream:

She is an owl wheeling above me. She asks, "Why do you want to fly with me?"

I am by the sea, labouring along the sandy beach, listening to the roaring waves.

"I want to fly with you because I'd be released."

She soars.

I run. I run through the city. I pass through the narrow, busy streets of the old town, the independent bookshops, the cafés, the small Victorian houses. I loop back to the sea. I can't hear the waves though I'm running in their surf. I crave their sound.

I return: "You make me want to live. I love your edge. You challenge me, you break through the defences I've constructed."

She alights on the branches of an oak, far above. A sigh returns to me in the wind.

I dart after her through thronging streets, but become unable to move. I am running but immobile, blocked by the sweat of dancing bodies crowding me, a hen party—high heels, stockinged legs, and raucous laughter, and a bride-to-be with a white veil to set off her open red bustier.

I find her, on a narrow, high wall, within reach.

"Being with you, flying with you, puts me in touch again with my desire. I have missed it. I love its energy. I feel that desire in my body. Desire to engage, to make contact."

She turns. I could reach out. I could touch her torn, tired feathers.

* * *

"So, what now?"

It's May. She sits opposite me. She has a drink. Coke with ice and lemon.

"I hate the way this story goes," I say.

"What, you mean the way it casts you as a lustful, ageing, would-be cuckold caught up in regret for lost opportunities and the terror of growing old; scared by the choices you have made—and have still to make—and terrified of their consequences?"

"No, please, say what you think, don't hold back." I pause. She doesn't smile. "It's an interpretation that asks no questions. It leaves me nowhere to go except dubious, temporary, pleasure and, sooner or later, indignity, loss, and pain. Mine and others'."

"Well, ask yourself some questions. The difficult ones. Quit your maudlin self-pity and think."

"I'm stuck. I can't think. Maybe it's the beers. Why are you here, anyway?"

"Why are *you* here? On your own in this hotel, in this isolated city, far from home? I'm here because you want me to be. Come on, think. Try these: What am I to you? What are my meanings? What is it in me you yearn for? Like the question that pious mentor asked of you, what is the nature of your desire?"

I'll just sit and stay quiet. Maybe she'll go away, leave me alone. I want her here and I don't.

"I'm working on it. But it's not clear. Maybe it's that I don't want the answers."

"Not good enough."

I allow myself to look up at her for the first time. Her eyes seem distant.

"Because it's not me you want," she continues, "not really. You know that, don't you? There's never a 'really.' There's always something more, or something else."[2]

"Yes, it is you," I object. "It's you. It's…but—if I could fly alongside you, with you, in your owl grace—I'd absorb your magic. In an instant. A different life. Youth."

She laughs, more than she needs to.

"I don't feel much like an owl. I'm not Christ either: you don't just touch my cloak and it's all better," she mocks, rising from the red-cushioned stool. There's pain in the slow straightening of her back. "You have to think. You have to listen. There's a long list to choose from: Butler, Lacan, Freud, Jung, Foucault, Cavarero, Jesus, whoever. Find someone you respect. What about Deleuze? And Guattari? You'd listen to them, wouldn't you?"

I hear her speak to someone behind me, at the bar. I turn and she's gone.

"Yes, listen to us." He's smaller than I imagined, with sideburns and filiform hair. He's taken her place. Next to him is the craggy, bespectacled, intense Guattari.

"It's not about her," Deleuze begins. "Desire is never only sexual nor only the individual's, if there is such a thing. And it has the potential to be productive."

"But it's me that feels it."

"Understand it as belonging to the social, the political, the economic—the *flow*, the 'multiplicity of libidinal currents'[3] that we experience and which becomes manifest in libidinal desire. Felix, you tell him."

"'It is by no means clear that desire has anything to do with objects. We're talking about machines, flows, levies, detachments, residues…. (W)e propose a positive conception of desire: a desire that produces, not a desire that is lacking.'"[4]

They both stare at me. They want a response. I can't speak.

A woman pulls up a chair to join them. Thirty-something, maybe; they greet her as Eve. I'm surrounded.

"What they're saying is, how is it that everything in your life suddenly feels as if it is not going as planned and predicted? How is it that you feel as if you're acting in ways that don't match what you think you intend? Are even at risk of betraying yourself? 'Desire, multiplicitous, complicated, paradoxical, is a way to begin to explain.'"[5]

"I wish I knew. I wish that made sense. It should do. Life should make sense."

"Tsk. Do we have to do all the work?" Guattari demands.

"Why not?" I ask. "You seem to know all the answers. Shit."

Eve again:

"You know this. You know it. For one, what, unconsciously, is your desire for May seeking to *produce*?"

"What do you most seek to create with/through the next phase of your life?" continues Deleuze. "What's being enacted in your desire that belongs not only to you but to others around you, the group, society? What else is going on in your world that might be symbolised in this longing?"

"Which could be? What?" Guattari pushes.

I try: "The need for change, perhaps. But I don't know what kind of change."

"It doesn't matter. You don't have to make it happen. You have to be aware, open. Your only—but heavy—responsibility is to be 'not unworthy of what happens to (you),'[6] to be open to the meanings that there might be and to allow for the movement and action that the unfolding of events might imply."[7]

"But that…that fills me with terror. I don't know what will happen. I don't know where it will lead."

"Yes, we know." There's a softness in Guattari's voice that I haven't noticed before. "That pain, that ache below your ribs, those dreams, May, your doubt. If you choose not to believe in the owl's magic, you will do the emotional work of answering the question of your desire."

Eve adds: "I believe that [y]our desire has expertise. In fact, I believe desire constitutes (y)our expertise."[8]

I slump. Enough. I don't know what they want of me.

I feel a touch on my shoulder, a hand resting, a gesture of compassion.

When I look up, they're all gone.

I've enquired after therapists. I've asked therapist friends for names of therapist friends I wouldn't know. I don't know if therapy is what I need but it feels familiar, something I understand. But I do not want to return to John. It has been 10 years since I last saw him, so maybe he has changed the glass door at the back of his house and found a way to deal with the musty, damp odour as you descend to his basement rooms. If I were to see him again:

I would ring the bell at the allotted time and not a moment before
He would not make eye contact with me
He would not speak until I was lying on the couch and had spoken first
He would sit behind my head
From the edge of my sightline I would see him reach down the glass at his feet

In the initial silence, I would seek the words
Seek the words
To give voice to what's there
He would stay silent then offer an insight I did not see coming
He would be without sentimentality
He would not be supportive
He would not be gentle
He would not even appear to be kind

I would return, twice a week, for as long as it took
I would hate him and love him
He would be steady and sharp and maddening

I would end with relief
I would reflect on him afterwards with affection and gratitude
When, years later, I heard a voice, I would turn to check if it was him
I would try to catch his eye
He would not acknowledge me
I would not know if he was keeping the boundaries clear
Or if he did not recognise me
I do not want to go back

I do not want to go back but I sense that I might. In the meantime I write. Perhaps I write, as Cixous (1991) and Atwood (2003) amongst others claim, to keep my (middle-aged sense of) mortality at bay.

Or I write to continue to inquire, to keep the puzzle breathing, to keep myself alive to the possibilities, to not close down, both for myself and so that I can continue to work with those men who hear their stories in mine.

I will be 50 in 8 weeks. It's a threshold I have to step across. I tell myself I have to work on accepting that ambivalence is a necessary condition of living and that, though I need to understand mine, it need not render me motionless. I determine to stay with the task of finding answers, or, at least, of understanding what the questions are.

* * *

She walks back into the hotel foyer and through to the bar. She's changed since finishing her shift and is on her way out to meet friends. Passing the cathedral just now, she had heard the wedding guests applauding on the steps as the bride and groom emerged.

She greets her colleague, who asks why she's returned.

"Oh, I forgot something. That's all."

She looks around. He's gone. Good. She had intended to tell him it was time to stop writing, and mischievously imagined taking his book from him, pretending to tear it up and ordering him to get out and live.

She returns to the summer evening sun outside, looks back and forth along the cobbled street, and spreads her wings.

Notes

1. *"Midway upon the journey of our life"*
2. See Frank, 1995
3. Deleuze and Guattari, 2004, p. 35
4. Deleuze, 2004, p. 223
5. Tuck, 2010, p. 639
6. Deleuze, 2004, p.169
7. Rajchman, 2000
8. Tuck, 2010, pp. 645-6

References

Atwood, M. (2003). *Negotiating with the dead: A writer on writing.* London: Virago.

Butler, J. (2005). *Giving an account of oneself.* New York: Fordham University Press.

Cixous, H. (1991). The last painting or the portrait of God. In D. Jenson (Ed.), *Coming to writing and other essays* (S. Cornell, D. Jenson, A. Liddle, & S. Sellers, Trans.). Cambridge, MA: Harvard University Press.

Clough, P. (1995). Problems of identity and method in the investigation of special educational needs. In P. Clough & L. Barton (Eds.), *Making difficulties: Research and the construction of special educational needs.* London: Paul Chapman.

Dante Alighieri (1975). *Inferno* (J.D. Sinclair, Trans.). Oxford: Oxford University Press.

Deleuze, G. (2004). *The logic of sense* (M. Lester, Trans.). London: Continuum.

Deleuze, G., & Guattari, F. (2004). *A thousand plateaus* (B. Massumi, Trans.). London: Continuum.

Erikson, E.H. (1959). *Identity and the life cycle.* New York: International Universities Press.

Frank, A. (1995). *The wounded storyteller: Body, illness, and ethics.* Chicago: University of Chicago Press.

Jackson, A., & Mazzei, L. (2008). Experience and "I" in autoethnography: A deconstruction. *International Review of Qualitative Research, 1*(3), 299–318.

Jaques, E. (1965). Death and the midlife crisis. *International Journal of Psycho-Analysis, 46,* 502–514.

Rajchman, J. (2000). *The Deleuze connections.* London: MIT Press.

Tuck, E. (2010). Breaking up with Deleuze: Desire and valuing the irreconcilable. *International Journal of Qualitative Studies in Education, 23*(5), 635–650.

Wyatt, J. (2005). A gentle going? An autoethnographic short story. *Qualitative Inquiry, 11*(5), 724–732.

Wyatt, J. (2008). No longer loss: Autoethnographic stammering. *Qualitative Inquiry, 14*(6), 955–967.

About the Authors

Durell Maurice Callier is a doctoral student in the department of Educational Policy Studies at the University of Illinois at Urbana-Champaign (UIUC). His research explores the relationships between Blackness, queerness, and spirituality by utilizing autoethnography, performative writing, and intersectional analysis indicative of Black feminist and queer cultural criticism. Currently, his research seeks to understand the pedagogical and political applications of performance to promote issues of social justice. This interdisciplinary scholarship contributes to the fields of gender and women's studies, queer studies, African American studies, performance studies, and qualitative research methodologies. An artist-scholar, Callier actively seeks to create scholarship which is deeply personal, politically spiritual, intrinsically accountable, and ultimately artistic.

Amira Davis is a mother, grandmother, community mother, artist and independent scholar. She holds an EdM in curriculum and instruction and a PhD in educational policy studies with a concentration in African American studies from the University of Illinois-Urbana. She did postdoctoral study in the Dept. of African American Studies—UIUC researching supplementary education in the U.S. and London. As a percussionist and poet, she has provided performances, programs and community-based educational projects for over 30 years. She has published several journal articles and book chapters. Her research interests include Black women's history and culture, Africana studies, critical theory and performance.

Marcelo Diversi is an associate professor of human development at the beautiful Vancouver campus of the Washington State University system. He continues to be haunted by humans' quickness in justifying the subjugation of the Other in the name of a higher moral ground, even when the cause is liberation.

Mitra Emad is an interdisciplinary scholar, trained in cultural anthropology at Rice University, a program long identified with experimental styles of ethnographic writing and cultural critique of social institutions. Dr. Emad teaches and writes about cultural constructions of the human body, especially in terms of how the body functions as a site for cultural translation. With a strong emphasis on engaged pedagogies, her work in the classroom is deeply tied with her research interests. She has published articles about the American comic book *Wonder Woman*, about the web discussion forum WITSENDO, and about cultural constructions of pain. She is currently completing a book, *Twirling the Needle: The Body as a Site for Cultural Translation in American Encounters with Acupuncture*, to be published by SUNY Press.

Dominique C. Hill, a scholar-artist and educator, is a doctoral candidate at the University of Illinois in education policy studies who uses dance and poetry to destabilize mis-readings of Black, youthful, and female bodies. For Dominique, dance is a personal signification of her life experiences and a communal vehicle of possibility and social transformation. Beginning her artistry at age nine in community centers and school expos in Buffalo, NY, her work is inspired by the women of her family and rooted by a passion to transgress boundaries. Her areas of interests are Black girlhood, arts activism, cultural issues in Education, and arts-based pedagogy.

Akil Houston is among a new generation of public intellectuals who merge public conversations with public service. An activist, educator, filmmaker, dj, social critic, and one of the nation's most authentic hip-hop scholars, Houston's research interests include mass media, education, gender, race, diversity, hip-hop culture, and youth. Houston is known for his thoughtful perspectives on everything from music to education to race. His respected commentary has been featured on NPR and newspapers throughout the nation. Houston serves as a member of the Hip Hop Congress National Leadership Council, advises the Ohio University local chapter and serves as an advisor to the Ohio University's Black Student Union. Currently, he is an assistant professor of African American Studies at Ohio University.

Susan V. Iverson is an associate professor of higher education administration and student personnel at Kent State University, and holds affiliate faculty status with both women's studies and LGBT studies. Iverson's research interests focus on: equity and diversity, status of women in higher education, critical pedagogy, and feminist and post-structuralist approaches to inquiry. Prior to becoming faculty, Iverson worked in student affairs administration for more than ten years.

Claudio Moreira is an assistant professor in the Department of Communication at the University of Massachusetts Amherst. He does performance autoethnography, always speaking up from the intersection of race, gender, and social class.

Elyse Lamm Pineau is associate professor of communication studies at Southern Illinois University, where she specializes in performance studies and communication pedagogy. Her research centers on performative autoethnography, directing for the stage, and critical arts-based pedagogies. In 2011, she was invited to the U.K. to present graduate seminars and conduct workshops at Plymouth University and the University of Bristol Graduate Schools of Education. Pineau has written and toured two one-person shows, and her work has been published in *Text and Performance Quarterly, American Educational Research Journal,* and *International Journal of Qualitative Inquiry.*

Jonathan Wyatt is head of professional development and a research fellow at the University of Oxford. He used to work a day a week as a counselor within the UK's National Health Service and now has a small private practice. Jonathan's research interests focus on writing and on the experience of loss, and his latest co-authored book is *How Writing Touches* (Cambridge Scholars, 2012). He lives in Abingdon, near Oxford, with his partner Tessa; their two adult children (Joe and Holly) are out in the world somewhere, making their way. Life's priorities feature coffee and football.

About the Editor

Mary E. Weems is a poet, playwright, performer, imagination-intellect theorist and Social Foundations scholar of urban education working in interpretive methods. She was the Poet Laureate of Cleveland Heights from (April 2007– April 2009). Weems is the author and/or co-editor of several books including *Cleveland Poetry Scenes: A Panorama & Anthology* (Bottom Dog Press, 2008), *Poetry Power* (Silvermoon Press, 2003), her educational text *Public Education and the Imagination-Intellect: I Speak from the Wound in My Mouth* (Peter Lang, 2003), *Working Hard for the Money: America's Working Poor in Stories, Poems, and Photos* (Bottom Dog Press, 2002), and a book of poems *An Unmistakable Shade of Red and the Obama Chronicles* (Bottom Dog Press, 2008). Weems book *For(e)closure* was a finalist in the 2011 Main Street Rag Poetry contest and is forthcoming from the MSR Press.

Weems has been widely published in journals including *The African American Review*, *Obsidian III*, and *xcp: Cross Cultural Poetics*. Her work has also appeared in numerous anthologies, most recently *Go, Tell Michelle: African American Women Write to the New First Lady* (SUNY Press), *Boomer Girls* (Iowa University Press), and *Spirit and Flame: An Anthology of African American Poetry* (SUNY Press).

Weems won the Wick Chapbook Award for her collection *white* in 1996, and in 1997 her play *Another Way to Dance* won the Chilcote award for The Most Innovative Play by an Ohio Playwright.

Mary Weems has had numerous articles, performance texts, and book chapters published in the field of education most recently: "Food for Thought: Empathy and the Imagination-Intellect" (2009), in the *Iowa Journal of Communication*, "The E in Poetry Stands for Empathy" (2009) in *Poetic Inquiry: Vibrant Voices in the Social Sciences* (Prendergast, Monica et. al. eds.), "Sadie Stories" in the *International Journal of Qualitative Studies in Education* Special Edition on Constructions of Childhood: Globalized Homelessness and Poverty (2012). Race is 'not' an Additive. Special Issue. Cultural Studies <> Critical Methodologies (2011).

Her plays and/or excerpts have been published or produced since 1997. In 2009 an excerpt of her play "At Last," which she performed with Dr. Elaine Richardson aka as Dr. E, was part of the Ingenuity Festival. Publications include "Another Way to Dance," and "Dead Soul 4413," part of *Another Way to Dance* and *Numbers* respectively published in *The Theatre Audition Book 2,* (Meriwether, 2009) Gerald Lee Ratliff, ed., and "Two Sides to Every Story," in *Still More Monologues for Women, By Women* (Heinemann Books, 2001), Tori Haring-Smith, ed. Currently Mary Weems is seeking production possibilities for her new play *Meat* which explores the murders of eleven Black women in her hometown and received a staged reading at the 2011 National Black Theatre Festival, and *Closure* which opened the 2010–11 season at the Karamu House, under the direction of Artistic Director, Terrence Spivey, with Dianne McIntyre as guest choreographer.

Mary Weems is currently an Assistant Professor in the Department of Education and Allied Studies at John Carroll University. She also works as a language-artist-scholar and Education consultant in middle school, and high school classrooms, university settings and other venues through her business *Bringing Words to Life*. For further information contact Mary Weems at mweems45@yahoo.com

 *General Editor: Norman K. Denzin*

Cultural Critique is a research monograph series drawing from those scholarly traditions in the social sciences and the humanities that are premised on critical, performance-based cultural studies agenda. Preference is given to experimental, risk-taking manuscripts that are at the intersection of interpretative theory, critical methodology, culture, media, history, biography, and social structure. Asserting that culture is best understood as a gendered performance, this international-research monograph series combines ethnography and critical textual approaches to the study of popular literature, media, myth, advertising, religion, science, cinema, television, and the new communication and information technologies. This new series creates a space for the study of those global cultural practices and forms that shape the meanings of self, identity, race, ethnicity, class, nationality, and gender in the contemporary world.

Preference will be given to authors who engage a variety of critical qualitative, interpretive methodologies, from semiotics and critical textual analysis to interpretive and auto-ethnography, personal narrative, and the practices of investigative, civic, intimate, and immersion journalism. We seek non-conventional, experimental manuscripts. Qualitative methods are material and interpretive practices. They do not stand outside politics and cultural criticism. Critical methodologies advance the project of moral criticism. This spirit, critically imagining and pursuing a more democratic society, has been a guiding feature of cultural studies from the very beginning. Contributors to the Cultural Critique series will forward this project. They will take up such methodological and moral issues as the local and global, text and context, voice, writing for the other, and the author presence in the text. Cultural Critique understands that the discourses of a critical, moral methodology are basic to any effort to reengage the promise of the social sciences for democracy in the twenty-first century. Cultural Critique publishes works of ethnopoetry, auto-ethnography, creative nonfiction, performance texts, book reviews, and critical analyses of current media representations and formations. Projected contents (and contributors) will be drawn from scholarly traditions in the social sciences and humanities, including history, anthropology, sociology, communications, art history, education, American studies, kinesiology, performance studies, and English. The scope of submissions will be international.

For additional information about this series or for the submission of manuscripts, please contact:

Dr. Norman K. Denzin
University of Illinois, Institute of Communications Research
228 Gregory Hall, 810 So. Wright Street
Urbana, IL 61801

To order other books in this series, please contact our Customer Service Department:

(800) 770-LANG (within the U.S.)
(212) 647-7706 (outside the U.S.)
(212) 647-7707 FAX

or browse online by series:

WWW.PETERLANG.COM